Vacatio...

Cash Flow Avalanche

Kelly T. Kortman

Publisher: Cedarbrook East, LLC.

Seattle, Washington

Contents

PREFACE

It was almost 6 years ago to the day back in 2007 when I purchased my first vacation property. And just like everybody else who's ever purchased a vacation home I knew very little about what it takes to successfully own and operate a vacation property let alone a vacation rental. As the economy faltered through the next couple of years I went from *wanting* to make a few extra bucks off of my property if I could to absolutely needing to generate as much rental revenue as possible so that I could make it through that economic downturn and come out on the other end still owning all of my real estate. It is truly amazing the things that we can accomplish when we have no choice but to accomplish them.

I was lucky in a few regards. Number one I had been a real estate agent back in the late nineties, so I had a bit of knowledge as it pertained to real estate. I was a financial advisor who had a fair amount of acumen as it pertained to real estate investment, most of which I had learned from my successful clients who they themselves had had successes in the real estate world. But mostly I had a sincere desire to succeed and come out a winner on the other end. I was willing to do whatever it took to make my property a success. And I can say without hesitation that the journey that I've been on has taught me just about everything that one needs to know to successfully own and operate a vacation rental, as I currently own one of the most successful and most oft rented and highly rated properties in the area that my property is in.

Whether you are purchasing a vacation property for the sake of investment and potential cash flow or you already own a vacation property and would now like to rent your property I feel in no uncertain terms that I can provide you with just about everything you could ever need to know so that you can be as successful with your property as I have with mine and so that you can run it by yourself thereby avoiding the massive fees that you often pay to have somebody else do it for you.

Now, I don't own dozens of properties. I own one property and I manage it extremely well. Would I like to have more properties down the road...perhaps. But I feel that you do not need to own 12 properties to be considered successful in this business in the same way that you don't need to own 12 sports franchises to be a successful sports franchise owner. Last I checked Robert Kraft only owned one football team, The New England Patriots and with that team had won several Super bowls. Me personally, I would rather own one football team and go to the Super bowl a bunch of times than own several major sports teams and have no championships (think Paul Allen who owns the Seahawks and Trailblazers).

As I go about telling my story I will include a few real life situations that I experienced. In my business as a financial advisor this is sometimes called "story-selling". But it does, in my opinion, help to create some perspective and it also breaks up the constant barrage of information.

Over these last 6 years I feel that there isn't much that I haven't come up against and therefore overcome. I was involved in absolutely every step of the process from start to finish and as a result consider myself to be an expert in running a vacation rental. The property that I currently own is one of the top rated properties in the area. I have never received less than a five star rating from any of the people who have rented my property and to me that says that I've done and am doing all of the right things. I am also always cash flow positive, (except for April, my slowest month) and when you consider that I bought my property at the top of the real estate market and am still cash flow positive every single month and sometimes double or even triple cash flow positive which to me suggests that I'm heading in the right direction.

And now it's my desire to share that wisdom, to help you to make your vacation rental as successful as possible from day one. To teach you everything I've learned about every aspect of the vacation rental process, from the very first day that you start looking for a property, if that be the case, to becoming as successful as you possibly can be in the day to day operations of running what I hope for you to be a very successful venture. I will also help you to avoid many of the mistakes that I made and trust me, when you are only left with the option of learning most everything as you go you are going to make mistakes. Then again it's going to force you to learn, to innovate and to create a system that is going to, over the long run, make you very successful as long as you don't give up, although it's my goal to help you to avoid as many of these potential pitfalls as possible

Without further ado let's begin with the first steps as we begin and continue forward from there.

Lastly, thank you for allowing me to help you.

Dedication

This book is dedicated to a few select people who have, in some way, inspired me throughout my life. In some cases it was just a comment or a phrase, in others it was their actions and deeds that I was fortunate enough to witness and for some it was the fact that they rolled the dice and took a chance on me. In no certain order here they are.

To my father, Donald Kortman, who taught me both the importance and the meaning of work ethic. He was an elevator construction worker and truth be told I do not ever recall him missing a day of work in his life.

To Dina Golab-Johnson who merely wrote in my Senior yearbook that I had a "great mind for business". I don't know how on earth she came to this conclusion at this point in my life but it was something that stuck with me and something I would have pinging around my head for 12 years before I ever really did anything about it.

People really do not understand the power of their words!

To Christian Zenger, the first true entrepreneur that I ever came in close contact with and who was a peer and a friend as opposed to a boss. He somehow instilled the belief in me that owning my own business was feasible and tangible. Prior to that I just thought that running your own business was something that was handed down from generation to generation, not something that a guy like me could ever really do. I've never seen the guy work for anybody but himself my whole time knowing him and that has also been inspirational.

I then have to thank those who gave me a hand up in this world and gave me a chance to make it in the business world when all that I had at the time was a lot of customer service skills and a ton of enthusiasm. So to Mark Poole who hired me to be a rookie trainee investment advisor for Morgan Stanley Dean Witter in early2000 and then to Shelley Frank who hired me to run a region for him at WaMu Investments in late 2001, without their belief in me I would not be writing this book today because I would have never gained the experience or the knowledge or frankly had made the income necessary to have done any of this.

I'd like to quickly thank my friend Bob Thompson for recognizing early in my career as an advisor that I was spending way too much money on depreciating and asked the question, "So, when are you going to start buying some *appreciating* assets?" That was a wakeup call and one which got me started in the real estate game in the first place.

I'd lastly like to thank all of my friends and family who have been listening to me for the past, probably, two years blather on about how I was writing a book. I'm sure most of you thought that you would never see it in print and to that I say, "there were many times that neither did I." But here it is, so there ya go.

*Interesting fact, 81% of US citizens think that they have a great idea for a book but only .01% of US citizens are actually published.

I also would like to thank you the reader for buying this book. Thanks for taking a chance on me! This book will remain a work in progress and please know that I wrote it and edited it and that although it may not be perfect yet, it will be some day. Know that I take comfort in the fact that even the Bible probably remained imperfect for a thousand years before they really got it perfectly written and edited.

1

Get rich schemes are just that" schemes" and most times they don't work

I know you've heard this before and perhaps you've seen this before. Everywhere you look, every library in the land and most late, late night commercials are filled with get rich quick schemes many of them involving real estate. The problem with all that is that I do not know anybody, personally, who has ever benefited from these schemes. Having been a financial advisor for the last twelve years I have had a chance to meet literally thousands of people who are very successful financially and not a single one of them has ever made a dime flipping real estate. I do know many who have tried but I do not know of anyone who has actually been successful at it.

1.

And if they ever did make a few bucks flipping properties when conditions were perfect they also, most likely, participated in the huge losses that were experienced during the real estate collapse of 2008.

Now I'm not taking anything away from those handful of individuals, wherever they are, who've found a loophole in the system and have found a way to make massive overnight profits in real estate, but those opportunities, for whatever reason do not seem to have found their way into my neck of the woods. There might be isolated parts of the country that during short periods of time afford these opportunities but my belief is that they are few and far between. I, for example, have a friend named Paul who has found a real estate imbalance in Texarkana, Texas. He has successfully been able to purchase homes in the 25-35k range that he has been able to turn around and rent for 700 dollars or sometimes even more per month. Obviously your positive net cash flow here is quite high if you can not only accomplish this feat once but 5 or 6 times over which he seems to have done. However, I've come to witness that sooner or later the secret will get out and things will come back into balance, either real estate prices will rise or rents will decline. In essence supply will eventually meet demand.

Although truth be told any market anywhere can become seriously overbought or oversold, in fact, real estate nationally went from being dramatically overbought in 2006 to dramatically oversold in 2009 and it seemingly happened almost overnight. As it turns out the best time to have actually purchased real estate would have been in 2009 or 2010 a time where most people either didn't want to invest in real estate, couldn't afford to purchase real estate due to the current economy or were still licking their wounds from the crash that occurred over the last few years. Perhaps the biggest factor though was just simply fear, fear that the market could or would continue to go yet lower proving once again that timing the market is not only hard but sometimes impossible.

2.

Real estate is bought and sold everyday, some at a loss and some at a profit by the current owner and or person who built it (or in special circumstances banks or municipalities that have taken the property into receivership). There are most certainly homes in foreclosure that are perhaps selling at a bargain to its fair market value but in an efficient marketplace it's hard to imagine an abundance of properties that can be bought and then sold for a huge profit in a very short period of time. It would seem that if these types of windfalls are occurring then I would be hearing about it, that or one of my clients or prospects would be in my office with a big fat check, at some point, getting ready to invest some of that easily found money. Yes it's true that we didn't experience a real estate bust here in Washington State anywhere near the level that we've seen elsewhere but we still do represent a microcosm of the US Real Estate market as a whole.

Now as I mentioned I have had the good fortune of sitting down in front of literally hundreds of high net worth people and truth be told I've met many of them who've done extremely well in real estate. But the people who have done well have done so by buying real estate and holding it for a very long period of time. I've also had the good fortune to sit down with folks who were divesting themselves of real estate and who were looking to invest in a diversified portfolio of stock and bond investments. Why would somebody sell a cash flow positive property for a stock and bond portfolio? Because owning real estate requires a fair amount of work. So let me point this out right now. There are no free lunches in real estate. Oh, I'm sure there are those that will argue with me and some of them might even be right, or lucky. But by and large owning real estate requires time, money and effort. And let me add one final point. There are two types of real estate owners. Slum lords who make up a small percentage of property ownership and then the rest of us, those of us who do all we can to bring the very best product to the market that we possibly can because in doing so we can then garner the highest amount of rent.

3.

Then there are those that create really great living environments for people and charge a fair rate only to find out 6 months later that they let a hoarder move in, or really in most cases people who move in and simply have no sense of how to take care of a home. And these people, maybe they let their pets run amok, maybe they end up with a leaky toilet that they let leak until the subfloor is completely rotted out or maybe they have parties featuring beer pong battles that last until the carpeting is soaked with alcohol and dirt.

Either way the money that they make in rent ends up being poured back into the rental to make it rentable again to the next group of possible nare do wells. Now although I don't ever hear stories about immediate windfall profits in real estate I do hear almost every day about renters who move out and leave a disaster for the landlord to clean up afterwards.

2

The benefits of a vacation rental property

Real estate is a great investment. There is no doubt about that. Every single piece of real estate out there is owned by somebody and whether you've purchased a second home for the purpose of having it be a rental or to live in from time to time yourself you still get to take advantage of many of the same benefits, although when owning a successful rental you get to experience so many other benefits and here are just a few:

Price Appreciation

The first benefit is probably also its most obvious. Investing in real estate and then watching it appreciate in value over time. This is obviously a great thing.

5.

The only problem with investing in real estate for this sole purpose is primarily capital gains taxes, real estate excise tax and realtor fees. Oftentimes, especially when trying to flip properties or fix and flip properties, all of these aforementioned costs can dramatically erode any short term profits you may have just made. Additionally once you sell the place where do you go next? Just like the stock market where all stocks typically rise on a great day in the market, home prices usually rise in conjunction with each other over time as well. So you sell a home at a profit only to purchase another home that was rising at the same rate as the one you just sold. Of course, as mentioned earlier, there are, from time to time, economic imbalances that exist or in other cases people fire selling real estate due to a death in the family or an unexpected job transfer, bankruptcies, foreclosures or simply a home that needs a lot of work but where there is value in fixing and then selling it once the remodel is complete.

An example of this was towards the very end of the real estate boom in 2006. Many folks who had successfully owned then sold real estate before the real estate collapse began were looking for the next great real estate opportunity.

There was a rumor abounding that Austin, Texas was going to be the place that was next on the list to move up dramatically in value. So folks who sold their properties at great prices in Florida, Las Vegas and Phoenix began to start looking around in Austin. But sadly Austin would end up experiencing declines in their real estate prices as well, maybe not as dramatic as Las Vegas but losses nonetheless.

The other problem with this style of investing is the very painful lesson that we learned in 2008. Not only do home prices not always go up, sometimes they go down and sometimes they go down so fast it can make your head spin and when you are leveraging that investment as most of us do

6.

(putting a small amount down and financing the rest of the "investment") then the percentage losses can be astounding.

Lastly, real estate is essentially illiquid in the very short term. I mean sure, at the peak of real estate bubbles and even during periods of relative real estate market normalcy you can buy a home, fix it up and then sell it down the road to a willing buyer and I would say that most often times the market works in this general fashion but even when times are good it can take anywhere from several weeks to several months to sell a home. I, for example, sold my home at the top of the market in 2005 and it still took 6 months and lowering the price by over 15+% to get it sold. If you are, however, buying real estate during a period where real estate is in bubble mode then you are going to have to rely on what is known as "The greater fool theory". This theory, essentially, is that you are going to pay way too high of a price for something in the hopes of selling it to an even greater fool at an even higher price. This is what occurred, for example, in Miami in the mid 2000's. Condo prices were rising dramatically due to national and perhaps even international interest in that market. What this created was a massive supply and demand imbalance. To counter steadily increasing demand the builders moved in and started creating an influx of inventory. Then as soon as this inventory would be put on the market there would be people standing outside in long lines with fat checks in their hands ready to get in on this "can't lose" proposition. That's the funny thing about bubbles and it doesn't matter what bubble it is that you are talking about, tech stocks in 1999, oil speculation in 2007, gold prices in 2011, people never want to get in when the prices are really cheap and the market for that particular asset is unloved, but boy do they love jumping in at the top and they almost always are left holding the bag. And this is when you know that a bubble is upon you and this is when you know to absolutely avoid an asset class.

7.

The secret is to never buy anything as an investment when the whole world is also lining up to buy it.

It would be my guess that the builders who were building properties near the peak of the bubble and who were able to sell out their properties at the top of the market did the best but I would also add that everybody was caught with their pants down when the market tanked in the 2006-2009 period and therefore it's also my guess that builders were deploying every ounce of capital that they had to purchase the next plot of land for their next amazing project at the market's peak or perhaps even slightly after the peak. Truth be told very few people are savvy enough to get out at the very height of a bubble and then just sit in cash. Businesses cannot make money sitting on cash and during the height of a bubble when you have employees to keep busy and overhead and other expenses to manage you have to keep moving forward with new projects and you have to keep deploying your capital and therein lies the rub for companies that develop real estate.

It would be at the point when real estate prices are in serious decline where real estate becomes the least liquid. Sure you can sell it for pennies on the dollar but really it's at this point that people walk away from the real estate investment losing all of their down payment and destroying their credit in the process.

From what I've seen and heard and witnessed the very best way to make money in real estate is to be a "buy and hold" investor, perhaps even taking advantage of leverage to both maximize your profits 4over time and purchase several properties or more thereby extrapolating the benefits of buying real estate for the long run. Here is a quick calculation for you that I know is going to sound improbably but will most likely turn out to be true due to the effects of inflation.

If real estate appreciates at a mere 4% per year (I'm predicting something closer to 6% over the next twenty years or so on average), which is an assumed average rate of return, then my $415,000 vacation rental is going to be worth 900,000 in twenty years when I turn 65.

That is a lot of coin especially when you compare it to the vast majority of Americans who will retire with little to nothing in their checking or savings accounts or 401k. I will take $900,000 any day over zero. Also by the time that we reach this milestone my cabin should be very close to being paid off and at that time I will be paying mostly principal.

Additionally if we assume 3% inflation as it pertains to the cost of living then the rent that I currently charge of $249 a night will be at $450 dollars a night twenty years from now.

If I'm still booking the place twenty nights a month then I'm looking at $9000 a month in revenue. That added to my $2,400 a month social security payment and hopefully also a stream of income coming from my 401k plan (placed into an IRA rollover account) and I'm sitting quite pretty and that's just from one property. Imagine if I can acquire another one or two more properties over the long run. $27,000 a month in income would be spectacular and that is the kind of money in retirement that allows all of your dreams to come true.

In conclusion there are many people who have made a living buying and selling real estate or fixing and flipping properties. But it takes more than skill to be successful with this, you also need to be pretty good at market timing and also have a bit of good luck. But there are certainly no sure things in this area of the market and I think that I have something far better.

9.

Rental Income

The next benefit would be, of course, watching rents rise over the years as a result of inflation so that over time your rental income payments far exceeds your mortgage payment or better yet, paying off your mortgage in 15 or 30 years (if you can avoid the constant refinancing and the pulling out of equity!) and then continuing to receive steadily rising rental income, which is still hopefully appreciating year over year (barring deflation, considered by most to be unlikely). And this is why they say that the first million dollars is the hardest to make, because once you own a few properties outright that are paying out a nice stream of rental income you will know firsthand what is meant by that statement. With the current US median home price hovering at around $50,000 it would actually take quite a string of homes to be a millionaire on paper. However, in California for example, the median price of a home is around $250,000, even after the most recent real estate crash. So less than a handful of homes owned and you would be well on your way to being a millionaire and with a strengthening rental market, homes of this value are currently kicking out some serious current income.

(How much to charge for rent, you ask?)

The general rule for how much to charge in monthly rent for a month to month lease is approximately 1.1% on a $100,000 home and then on a sliding scale downward as the rental property you are purchasing increases in value as the rental clients for those more expensive homes begins to diminish.

Therefore a $100,000 home would collect around $1,100 dollars per month which isn't a bad deal when you consider that your mortgage on that property (if you have one) is probably going to be around $710 dollars per month on a no money down loan at 4% fixed over 30 years.

(if you can still get that, especially on a second home).

So clearly being $390 dollars per month positive cash flow is a great thing especially when you consider the tax benefits of owning rental property but I still believe that it cannot come close to an effectively managed vacation rental.

That said I charge $249 dollars a night weekends and slightly less than that (199 dollars) on the weeknights for a home that I purchased for $400,000 in 2007. I charge more during the holidays ($330 and up). So if we do the math on my vacation rental if I was renting out my place by the month I could expect to receive approximately $3,200 dollars per month. (Using a sliding scale and adjusting down from 1.1% to about .08%). However based on the fact that I'm averaging closer to $225 per night and renting out my place between 20-25 days per night I'm bringing in in excess of $4500 and sometimes as much as $5,500 or more. And considering that everything does come out in the wash I have sometimes found myself renting every single day in December and January whereas certain months like April or May I might be lucky to get only the weekends rented out. Again, though, if you average it all out it can end up being over 20 days per month.

Tax benefits

Also, and something which will be covered in depth in a later chapter is the outstanding tax benefits that can be derived from owning real estate. But in a nutshell; mortgage interest, business expenses and depreciation are all items that can dramatically reduce how much you are taxed on your current income in certain circumstances.

Leverage

Another well-known fact is that the more you can borrow from a bank when purchasing real estate the greater your rate of return (or loss, of course) on a property is as it appreciates (or depreciates) in value.

Simply put if you put 10% down on a home and that home rises in value by 10% your rate of return isn't merely 10% - it's 100% because you just made back what you put into the property and based on the historical rate of return of real estate most investors have a chance to make approximately that rate of return about every two years depending on a host of factors like location, supply and demand and whether your city or state is seeing rising or falling population relative to the amount of buildable land in the area. For example while Detroit is seeing declining population Phoenix is seeing a population boom and the end result is rising prices in Phoenix while Detroit's real estate prices have collapsed.

Vacation Rental Income vs. Typical Rental Income

I will take nothing away from those who occasionally hit the real estate lottery. Those who've found some great little niche, whether that is buying super distressed properties and nursing them back to health or those who have an inside track on purchasing bank foreclosures for pennies on the dollar.

I can only go for what I know and what I do know is that a great number of my clients have done well in real estate through owning residential or commercial property again over a very long period of time and as you can see from the following equation it wasn't really the real estate itself (although choosing the right home at the right price in the right location is a critical component,

12.

I don't want to diminish that) that was the key ingredient in their success but really it was more so compound inflation and here is some basic math that explains what I mean by that.

A house purchased in 1950 at the median price of $9,000 growing at 6% over the last 60 years would be worth $296,000 today or almost a 30 fold increase. Sounds about right though, doesn't it? Ask your grandparents what they paid for their first home and then ask them what it is worth now, if they still own it. Most will give you similar figures unless it was beachfront property purchased in La Jolla when San Diego was an out of the way, sleepy, little fishing village way back in the day.

Additionally the rate of return is even more exponential when you consider that all that was required to purchase this home was a down payment of $1800 and payments of $57 a month. I mean it seems like a miracle when you hear stories about a 30 fold increase like this but it's really just simple math. And this is not to mention that almost every one of those early fifties era homes (2 bedrooms, 1 bath, kitchen and family room) have been extensively remodeled and added onto which has also helped to add to the value. So, yes, inflation and compound interest are your best friends when you own real estate. And so really it's not real estate that is the miracle here, really, again its compound interest (sometimes called the eight wonder of the world) that is the real miracle in this equation.

Now, like me, I've had clients buy the cassette tapes, the books and attend the seminars about getting rich in real estate, I've had clients bidding for foreclosures through banks and on the courthouse steps and simply put I cannot think of a single person that got wealthy this way but I can cite hundreds of examples of clients who became wealthy buying real estate the old fashioned way, by buying and holding real estate for the long term.

13.

The cash flow king: Vacation Property Rental

As good as real estate can be over the long run I truly believe that nothing has greater potential then an effectively managed vacation rental, and for so many reasons. The main reason though is having the ability to charge by the night as opposed to by the month. There is no way that you are going to charge somebody $6,000 a month to rent a $400,000 home but by charging somebody $200 a night and by getting that property booked almost every single night of that month, well, you have now accomplished nothing less than just that.

I will also add that to attempt to do this requires a little bit of the gambler mentality. Of course by charging by the month and making the renter sign a 6 month or 12 month lease you can budget things out very nicely and know what your income is going to be and really not have to worry about anything till you have to find a new renter next year or even further down the road if the renter continues to live at your property, which many renters usually prefer to do because, after all, who enjoys packing and moving every 12 months? (Also, if a landlord finally, finally gets a not-horrible renter they are prone to let them continue to live there at the same basic amount of rent for fear of tipping the apple cart, the devil you know is oftentimes better than the devil that you don't!) I mean the last time I moved into my last house I swore I was never going to move again and short of winning the lottery I very well might live out that promise.

In that regard buying a property in that vein and renting it out on those terms is like having a nice steady salaried government job. However, renting out your place by the night means constantly working, advertising, negotiating, selling and dealing with contracts.

14.

That said, some of the highest earners I know are those who chose to forgo the annual salary or the hourly wage and go into fully commissioned sales. There is no higher paying job than that of a fully commissioned salesperson at the top of their game. It doesn't matter if you are selling real estate, investments, fax machines or widgets.

Your income is only limited by the limitations that you put on yourself. Even in my own industry of financial services I have peers who make as little as $40,000 a year and those who make over a million dollars a year doing the same thing for the same bank but at a different bank location. Sure they might work at a different branch and have different skill sets but they all have the same opportunity. Really it's about talent, skill, desire, work ethic. A vacation rental is no different. The right property, with an attractive design in a good location with a decent owner behind it can do extremely well.

With a vacation rental the rewards are therefore substantially higher. And in addition to the rewards you still have a place that you can go hang out at at your leisure (although you will find yourself forsaking your own vacation time in lieu of revenue!) You also get to have your cleaner in there after every stay so you are never going to walk into a rental where your renter has just moved out and you come to find rotting bathroom floors, a stainless steel kitchen stove that needs to either be sandblasted or simply thrown away because it's caked with burnt on foods or carpets so saturated with filth or pet stains that you merely have to roll it up and throw it away. All of those things take money and time but more importantly cut into your profits. A single month that goes by without a renter can seriously impact your cash flow for the entire year and while you are missing out on revenue you are also sometimes spending a ton of money at Home Depot and Empire Carpet trying to make the place rentable again. And as you hand the keys to your newest renter you just close your eyes and pray that they aren't going to turn out to be as bad as the last one.

15.

Another analogy that I use when discussing the benefits of a nightly rental as it pertains to the income potential is that of a rental car.... If you buy a car from an auto dealership and agree to a 199 dollar a month lease payment and then turn around and rent that car out at 49 dollars a day and keep that car rented most of the month you can see how you can generate significant positive cash flow from that rental car. The secret to getting as much revenue off of that car as possible though is pretty simple. Keep your overhead low, keep your maintenance up and buy a decent car that people are going to want to rent in the first place and market and advertise it well.

When I bought my vacation home in 2007 if you were to have told me then that it would be generating some $4000-$6000 per month I would have told you that you were crazy (I even had a month where I generated over $8000 in income, because when you are doing bookings you are not always doing bookings just for that month, sometimes you are doing bookings for weekends that are weeks or months down the road). But sure as I stand here today that is what has become the case.

Now we know what works and what is feasible. Now the question is. How do we go about it? And the answer would be, not the way that I went about it. Yes, I did a lot of things well and got a lot of things right and also got quite lucky. But almost everything else that I've learned I've learned through trial and error and let me tell you the trial part can be time consuming and the error portion can be costly. My hope is that this book, this *guide,* so to speak can help you to accomplish all that I have accomplished and more but without all the costly mistakes and lessons learned.

Now whether you already have a vacation home that you would like to turn into a vacation rental or if you have a vacation rental right now that is underperforming I truly feel that I can help you to maximize that property's potential.

16.

I feel in no uncertain terms that I have created a streamlined system that will allow you to get the most web traffic possible, have the most people possible viewing your property and upon finding your property - arriving at a place that is beyond adequate, appropriately decorated, priced right for the particular time of year and in relation to what you are bringing to the table and set up in such a way that locking them in and booking them is as easy as one, two, three.

In the pages that follow I am going to show you everything that I've done to create the success that I have with my rental today. I am going to show you how to find the property if you haven't already. If you've already found or own your property I'm going to show you how to ensure you are renting it as often as possible and getting the best price per night that you possibly can and also generating the most revenue possible per month. Once you find your rental I am going to give you suggestions on how to appoint it, how to decorate it in line with what people today are looking for. I'm going to then show you how to advertise it and market it, how to negotiate pricing and how to seal a deal with a potential guest and then finally how to easily secure contracts and security deposits with very little effort on your part.

What I mainly hope to do, beyond making sure that your vacation property is perfectly aligned to do as well as possible is to also show you how to cut out the middleman. The firm, or person or agency whose agenda it is to make as much money off of your property as possible, money that could be going into your pocket instead of theirs. Middlemen in the vacation rental business, because it can be construed as so hands on, can and will try to take as much as half of your profits (a quarter if you are lucky) if you allow them to. I also feel that if you allow them to then you may be defeating the purpose of having a vacation rental in the first place as they will take so much of your profit that it won't be much better in the end than just renting it out by the month.

A word to the wise as well, though, creating the perfect vacation rental isn't necessarily cheap or easy and could create some up-front costs, also there will be legwork involved in getting your whole process streamlined, but once you get to that point, as I am now, I truly believe that if you follow my advice you will be able to achieve the same success that I've been able to achieve.

Towards the end I will provide a troubleshooting guide so that you will always have a handbook nearby so that you know how to deal with all of the various guest issues that might arise when owning and renting a vacation property.

Getting to where I got today wasn't easy but it sure is nice today. And although I'm not the owner of an abundance of rental properties, nor may I ever wish to be, seeing as one of my goals for this life is happiness and simplicity I have been able to hone my skills in the vacation rental arena and become somewhat of an expert at it.

This streamlined process is also able to be extrapolated and duplicable, meaning, done correctly you can manage many properties with this system and as I often say lif I did have 3 of these properties I might never have to work for anybody else ever again and the best job you can ever have is one that you simply do not need and therefore could walk away from at any time.

3

Getting Started

<u>My background</u>

I guess you could say that I've been around the block a few times. I've been a licensed real estate agent giving me some experience and background in real estate, I've been a financial advisor for the last 12 years which has given me an extensive background in investments and I've interviewed literally thousands of high net worth individuals giving me a ton of insight into what has worked for my clients and what hasn't. And to me an investment is an investment is an investment. It doesn't matter if it's gold or oil or a stock or even real estate.

The investment is both sound and inexpensive in the moment, on a relative basis, or it is not. There is no middle ground.

I've also worked in a bank for the last 10 years doing investments so I also have been around mortgages and the financing of real estate indirectly. Therefore, I feel that I'm skilled in a couple of very important areas when it comes to real estate as an investment. I'd like to think that I know a good deal when I see one and I understand some of the complexities of the financial world. I have a pretty good idea of the price of things. I've travelled a lot so I know what one should pay for a night at a given establishment. As a former real estate agent I understand real estate, real estate pricing, financing, contracts, negotiations and so forth. As a financial advisor I understand things like supply and demand, running a business, quite a bit about the complexities of taxes and how they relate to real estate. Also, again, having had the pleasure to meet many clients and prospects I know that real estate can be a great part of a client's financial plan. Later I will talk about what I've learned from my clients regarding leverage, using other people's money (via bank loans), mortgage interest tax deductions and depreciation. There are so many great things about real estate, especially as it pertains to vacation rentals that I couldn't possibly list them all here but will in later chapters.

Beyond having a few levels of expertise in the financial part of this business; because of my extensive customer service background, I also know a thing or two about customer service, which is a very important part of this business when it comes to dealing with guests. One of the goals of this book is to help you to be able to run this business from end to end in your spare time, except for perhaps the need to hire a cleaner to clean your property in between rentals. Therefore being able to deal with the travelling public is very important.

I also feel fortunate to have a bit of an interest in interior design and I've used many of the professional's tricks to deck out my rental with much less money than you would think if you were to walk into my property.

All of these attributes added together have helped me to turn my vacation rental into what it is today and that is one of the busiest and most profitable vacation rentals in the area that I operate it in. But it doesn't matter where your property is, if there are hotels nearby then you have a chance to be successful. Of course the better your location is the more successful you will probably be and yes, I'm sure there are places that simply wouldn't work for a vacation rental (a few places come to mind) but if you purchased a vacation property it must have been for a very good reason that you chose the location that you did and therefore I'm sure we will be able to work with it. If you've already chosen your location you can skim over the next chapter, if you haven't then please read on.

Attaining financing

Bank financing

Before beginning your search for the perfect vacation property it's best to get prequalified. Talk to a banker or a mortgage broker about what you can afford, how much you have to putdown, etc. etc. Know your price point before you begin the search, obviously.

To the best of my knowledge you are going to need to have perhaps as much as 20-25% down when purchasing a second home and then you are going to need a fair amount of capital to get your rental property established.

A quick ball-park guess is going to be around at least $20,000 for end to end furnishings down to the last wash cloth depending upon the size and how skilled you are at finding bargains.

This figure also takes into consideration the purchase of a hot-tub and some of the other amenities we've discussed. So if you are thinking about buying a $250,000 place for example, (which would seem about right for the average vacation rental taking into consideration that people like to vacation in nice, desirable and therefore more expensive places) you are going to need to have about $60,000 to $80,000 in readily available capital. It might also take you some time to get this rental off the ground and build a client base so it would make sense to have 6 months' worth of mortgage payments in the bank or a really great current income before you move forward with the purchase as well.

When I purchased my cabin in 2007 the timing couldn't have been simultaneously more perfect and at the same time more terrible. Although there were tiny cracks starting to show in the metaphorical dam that was the housing market at that time nobody had really caught on to how bad the market would become. Banks were still doing crazy loans, real estate appraisers were being very generous with their assessments of the properties that they were appraising and buying a second property was a piece of cake. I simply pulled money out of my primary residence which had gone up in value like crazy over the last year and used that money to put 10% down on the cabin I was buying up in the mountains. I remodeled the cabin with what was left over and when those funds ran out I simply tapped into a line of credit I had with American General (a subsidiary at that time of AIG, go figure). All told I ended up spending $41,000 for the down payment, $8,000 for furnishings etc. $3,000 for renovations , $5000 for a hottub and $20,000 for a new driveway. Grand total $77,000.

22.

Nowadays I would need that much money just for the down payment. Times have certainly changed!

How much home can I qualify for?

Assuming that you have good credit the general rule of thumb is that you can afford a payment that is no greater than 28% of your total monthly income and your total obligations may not exceed 36% of your total income.

Here is a simple calculation that illustrates this. Let's assume that you make $200,000 a year and you already own a primary residence worth $250,000 at say 4% interest and now you would like to purchase a rental property. How much can you afford assuming you have no credit card debt and let's say a $400 car payment.

The calculation would look something like this:

Monthly gross income	$16,667
Front-end ratio	28%
Calculated payment for front-end ratio	$4,667

Back-End Ratio

Debts and obligations	$1,600
Percent of gross income	10%
Maximum percentage available for mortgage payment	26%
Calculated payment for back-end ratio	$4,400

Payment Calculation

Minimum of the two ratio options	$4,400
Less: taxes and insurance	$125
Equals: maximum allowable payment	$4,275
Calculated mortgage amount	$796,354
Down payment	$20,000
Home value you can afford	**$816,354**

As you can see in this scenario at the current rates assuming a 30 year fixed mortgage you can afford a lot of house. Word to the wise though based on my experiences through the financial crisis of 2008. Purchase half the home that you can afford, there is no need to buy something that is going to eat up every dollar of your disposable income. Even if you have a slew of money in savings you can watch that quickly erode in an unfortunate market environment. Once that rental is fully established you can always go out and try to qualify for another one!

Seller financing

If there isn't any way that you are going to get a loan from a bank then your next bet would be to look into seller financing. Very simply, seller financing would be where a homeowner, (typically one who no longer has a mortgage) will act as the bank and sell you the home and in return you would make your interest and principal payments to them for a certain period of time or until you can attain bank financing. If for some reason you can no longer make the monthly payments the seller would simply take the home back and usually what you have paid in up to that point becomes considered rental payments. Because seller financing doesn't normally require qualifying for the loan it is a way that would allow you to purchase a vacation property when no other way is available. This also works out quite well for the seller in a market where he has a home he desperately wants off of his books but cannot find a buyer for through conventional means, this also works well for lower priced properties.

In addition to conventional financing and seller financing I'm sure there are a lot of other ways to get a deal done. Partnering with somebody and then providing sweat equity and a host of other ideas.

This isn't really a book about how to finance real estate but I will say that in this day and age it's a lot harder to purchase a second home than it used to be and more often than not you will have to qualify based on your current income, specifically what is on your tax return.

Also, if you cannot afford to make the mortgage payment out of your current income then you might not wish to move forward with the vacation rental. Relying on rental income to make your entire monthly obligation from day one is a risky bet. There will be slow months, especially in the beginning and if you are counting on rental income to make your mortgage and it simply isn't there then you are going to run into cash flow issues galore and I will tell you right now there is nothing worse than having more bills than income or depleting hard earned savings to keep a vacation rental afloat.

Locating the perfect vacation rental

First know what you want

When I began the search for my vacation property I wasn't necessarily thinking about finding a vacation rental. I was merely looking for a great little place that I could afford that would hopefully go up in value over time and add tidily to my retirement plan. I had a number of goals in mind when purchasing my place and some of those goals were as follows:

I wanted a place in the mountains, I wanted a cabin, I wanted something rustic on some land, I wanted to be near a pretty cool little mountain town, I did not wish to be near some tourist trap town, (although most towns are what you make of them, Waikiki can be a tourist trap or it can be a super relaxed vacation spot with tons of free activities, like surfing or hiking, really it's what you make of it)

25.

I wanted a town that purported itself to be active so that I could embark on all that the town had to offer from an outdoors standpoint. I wanted beauty and a view. I wanted something that was appropriately priced and a tiny bit of a fixer upper so that I could add my own sense of character to the property and with that I feel that I succeeded in every category. I would have loved to have purchased something on the water but that was not going to be a possibility considering that I was buying into what turned out to be the tippy top of the real estate market.

That said, I also was very lucky to buy into a market that turned out to only be about 7% overpriced due to the real estate bubble as opposed to some markets that were overpriced by 100% or more (I'm looking at you Miami and Las Vegas). I chalk the bulk of that good fortune up to nothing more than luck.

Back in the fall of 2007 the stock market was performing very well. Being a seasoned financial advisor I was doing quite well right along with it. With the good fortune of having money to spare and already having what I felt to be enough in the stock market and unable to get a decent yield from money markets or CDs, I began my search for the perfect vacation property. As many of my clients have stated, real estate is tangible, you can touch it, see it and even live in it if you have to. What many of my clients forgot however is that real estate can experience price volatility and moments of illiquidity. It does remain, however, a nice piece of the pie in a well thought out financial plan.

Living in Seattle, where it rains a lot, I wanted a place on the other side of the mountains, which has a much drier climate. I wanted to be near a ski resort if possible and also near some attractive fresh water lakes. Leavenworth seemed to offer all of that. Leavenworth, Washington, for the record, is a bustling little mountain town about 40 minutes past the top of the mountain pass that separates Seattle from Eastern Washington.

26.

Leavenworth is also very close to Steven's Pass Ski resort which is, in my opinion, one of the best ski resorts in the state.

Every major city has its own little "Leavenworth". If you live in Chicago, for example, it might be the Wisconsin Dells, if you live in Phoenix it might be Sedona, if you live in San Francisco it might be Calistoga and if you live in Houston it might be Galveston or New Braunfels. But every major city has that amazing place a few hours away that everybody wants to spend time at. And that is where you need to begin and possibly end your search.

After pinpointing where I wanted to purchase a property I called a real estate agent who operated out of Leavenworth and who had a focus on cabins, vacation properties and higher end properties.

After getting qualified by the bank as to what I could afford I drove out to Leavenworth one sunny August weekend in 2007 and as should be the case my realtor, Dwight, had a list of five or so properties that were available at the time for me to look at.

<u>My day with a Realtor</u>

As I followed him through this beautiful country I was in awe of the splendor of the day and immediately knew that I had chosen the right location. When I had left Seattle it was a typically weird August afternoon, 58 degrees and cloudy. Seattle is unique in that it can be 90 one day and then 55 the next if the clouds roll in and if there is a slight breeze coming out of Canada. However as I came over the pass and started making my way down the mountain the clouds turned to fog which turned to mist which turned to scattered clouds and then full out sun. The temperature rose into the high eighties (this is Alpine country after all) and Lake Wenatchee sparkled in the midday sun.

Just as the realtor had suggested we met at a small gas station just out of town and soon were on our way to look at our first property.

I, again, knew that I was going to be making an offer that weekend and I couldn't wait to have that magic moment when the property that would become my destiny would first come into view. The thing about me is that I don't shuffle my feet on stuff, when I decided to do something I do it.

The first place that we arrived at was quite nice but near a slow running river in the deep woods. Therefore there were mosquitos everywhere and even in the heat of the day I got bit several times. The cabin was also down a long dirt road where it would appear that I might have to be responsible for plowing in the winter which, for me, was not going to work and would probably be fairly cost prohibitive. So therefore I knew right away that that place was out of the question.

The next place that we went to was on fast running river and although wooded was more open and drier, therefore no mosquitos. However, it was going to need a new deck, landscaping, new carpeting, bathroom and kitchen updates and a lot of other work. It was a big rustic cabin though with a lot of character but I wasn't ready to spend that kind of money on a complete remodel. Plus being large and on the river it was pretty spendy to begin with but it also had no land and had neighbors really close by on both sides.

After packing it up there we finally came upon a really great opportunity. Sitting way up on a hill and overlooking Lake Wenatchee was this gorgeous little cabin with a lot of potential. Sadly though, although it was newer it was badly in need of a lot of exterior work. As we walked up the creaky stairs and onto the deck that overlooked all of Lake Wenatchee I immediately saw that the very large deck was probably going to need to be completely replaced. Cedar is a very pretty wood but if you don't stain it often it just crumbles and falls apart in the heat of the sun and this is what was happening here.

28.

The deck and railings were disintegrating and most likely would need to be replaced and that would be expensive.

The inside however was loaded with potential. It was laid out very nice but still needed a lot of cosmetic work and it also had some unfinished rooms downstairs. These rooms were framed and the infrastructure was in but the drywall and doors and so forth hadn't been finished. This is the kind of stuff that can be a gold mine. The trivial stuff that people with no vision looks at and dismiss as being difficult to fix when really it's the most easily fixed.

I walked around noticing that the place was most likely currently being rented by some young college kids or perhaps a bunch of ski instructors, despite efforts to clean up for our visit the place still had that college party vibe thing happening, the furniture was old and haphazard, it smelled like beer and just generally seemed dirty. Of course I could look past all that stuff if the price was right and without question it was as it was going for somewhere in the mid 300's. (Word of note here, when going into the vacation rental business better to have three300k cabins than one million dollar cabin as million dollar cabins are very hard to rent at the price that you would expect and really need to bring in to ever get to cash flow positive.) As the day turned to late afternoon I felt like I had found the first place that I wished to put an offer in on.

After discussing this with my realtor he suggested that I take a look at one more place before we called it a day. Even though I felt relatively fixed on the last place that I had just seen I decided that it made sense to continue forward.

29.

The Discovery on Eagle Creek

I followed him in my car, dogs happily sniffing the wind in the back of my Jeep, as we meandered through the town of Plain and up the Chumstick Highway until we came to a little road called Eagle Creek. Before I knew it and after having just passed a winery we came upon a nice sized cabin, not too big, not too small and which had a lot of fine attributes. It sat on 9 mountainous acres whereas the other cabin was on around a half an acre, the cabin owned a mountaintop which I also thought was pretty cool, the place also had that strange effect in that it seemed much larger on the inside than from the outside due to the fact that it had a peaked roof, a loft and a kitchen and living room area that went all the way to the ceiling.

The whole interior seemed to be literally covered in pine and offered up that cathedral effect because of the pitch of the roof and being able to see all the way to the ceiling made it seem perhaps much larger than it really was. There was also a very nice deck, a wood burning, cobblestone fireplace a nice kitchen and a rather large master bedroom. The value added however was this it was so much closer to the center of the town of Leavenworth where most everything happens. It was a real toss up, but for me I had to go with the property with the view of Lake Wenatchee first. The thought of sitting out there on that deck at night drinking a beer and looking out on the water as the sun set seemed like a fantasy come true. Also being the type of person that once I decide that I'm going to do something I do it, therefore, I decided to put in a second offer on the property on Eagle Creek. I am very much a believer in destiny and I felt and still feel today that I was in the market at that time because that was my destiny.

Interestingly enough even though nobody had put in an offer on my first choice in months one seemingly came through the fax moments before my offer came through and being a full price offer it was immediately accepted.

30.

On the second property on Eagle Creek I had made an offer some $60,000 dollars below asking price and lo and behold it was immediately accepted by the selling party. And so it was done. I was now the proud owner of a second home, a vacation property and my journey was about to begin.

Finding your own property

As I conclude this chapter I would like to give you some tips and pointers for finding your own vacation property.

<u>Location</u>

Location is obviously critical. Find a place that is maybe several hours from your home, not so far away that you never want to go there but not so close that it really doesn't feel like you are on vacation or at the very least, out of town. Try to be near water if you can. Obviously most people on vacation like being near water, whether that is to swim, fish, boat, canoe or whatever. Being near water is, in most cases, well enough. You don't have to be right on the water to be happy or successful and honestly the added price and taxes and even the liability that come with water property might not even make it worth it unless you have a ton of disposable income. Water is also dangerous on so many levels. Some parents might fear their young child walking out the front door and into the lake or getting tugged out by a wave or walking down to a river and getting grabbed by a current. Children are fascinated by water and parents on vacation are oftentimes busy managing any number of tasks. So near water but not directly on water can have many advantages.

<u>Condo vs. Single family</u>

Having some land is helpful. Giving people some room to move around is nice.

I will also add that condominiums and townhomes can reduce your profit potential due to the homeowners dues associated with them. Vacationers also have a tendency to let loose a bit. Even when you attract the right crowd vacationers like to drink, play games, be high spirited and therefore be pretty loud. God forbid that you have a townhome or condominium next to folks who live in the unit year around, you will never hear the end of it as it pertains to noise complaints (and therefore fines) and you also aren't going to have security readily available to deal with it. A home-owners association serves many functions and one of those functions is to provide a safe, quiet and happy environment for their tenants.

If you continue to be out of compliance with the HOA as a result of noise complaints you are going to find yourself paying higher and more frequent fines. You may find yourself forced to sit in on a variety of HOA hearings held in your honor. Also, if your CC &R's do not allow for vacation rental activity you can find yourself in real trouble. If you think you are going to get away with having an illegal vacation rental you are only kidding yourself.

The gig will be up sooner than you could possibly imagine and then you are back to square one. Condos can also at times offer less in the way of appreciation and resale value. Not always but sometimes and if homeowners dues start to run away from you as I've seen from time to time you can find yourself in quite a bit of cash flow trouble. Special one-time assessments can also erode your profits at the worst time possible. If an HOA doesn't prepare for upcoming projects and one becomes necessary (driveway paving, siding, paint overhaul, etc.) you could find yourself on the hook for a proportional percentage of repairs.

An aside on Time share vacations/rentals

If you are contemplating a time share vacation, stop. Simply put, I wouldn't do it. Number one it will probably never turn a profit. The thing about an investment is that you make money from taking advantage of supply and demand. When demand outstrips supply prices rise, however, with time share vacations there is what seems to be an unlimited supply and supply will always, it seems, be created at the same rate or even greater than existing demand. Therefore you will probably never sell your time share in the future to somebody else at a profit. It's just very unlikely.

When purchasing the time share you are first going to pay for the time share itself. The price can vary wildly depending mostly on how gullible you are.

If you've ever been to a time-share presentation you might full well know the high pressure sales tactics they use to get you to buy. (I've been to two, one time I literally wasn't allowed to leave the room until the presentation was over and at another in Cabo San Lucas I was literally bullied and belittled when I told them flat out I wasn't going to purchase the time share) both times I went to the presentations for the free activities they offer which sometimes can be really nice like horseback riding, ATV's, surf lessons, whale watching and so forth.

Now if you don't purchase the time share during the first presentation oftentimes you are forced into a second presentation where they offer you all the same stuff but for a much cheaper price. How can they do this? For the same reason that gyms sell thousands of memberships at a gym that can only hold a hundred or so people at one time. The reason is that oftentimes people buy the timeshare but then never use it or they use it sporadically or they do sometimes actually create more supply.

Once you purchase the time share then there are annual maintenance fees and if you actually use your time at the time share you often get hit with cleaning fees and restocking fees which makes the choice to simply just stay in a nice hotel (if that's what you really wish to do) a much better choice or option.

Purchase something that lends itself to the area

Also as it pertains to location and property, try to cater as best you can to the area that you are renting in. People on the beach love "beach houses" people in the mountains love cabins, people out in the country like that farmhouse vibe and people in the city might be looking for a metropolitan feel. The list goes on and on. Now when you make your purchase it doesn't have to look like that immediately but if that is the case you had best be prepared to do some fairly significant overhaul. Also, purchase what you can afford. If all you can afford is a higher end manufactured or small stick built home then do that but spend what you can to provide it with the absolute best vibe that you can that fits with the local area.

Size

As I mentioned earlier size is important but my belief is that smaller or mid-size is better than huge. Now if you can afford huge and are looking for some income from the property then go big. My friends and I sometimes get together and rent these spectacular mansions and with 14 of us pitching in the total cost is fairly economical. But you are going to have a harder time finding guests who can afford $1,200 a night and you are also always going to be dealing with rather large groups of people normally and when large groups get together chaos typically ensues. Being respectful guests,

34.

my crew and I do a massive clean-up on the last day prior to checkout but we've almost always given up a portion of our security deposit upon checking out because something almost always doesn't come all the way clean or something almost always gets broken. It's the cause and effect of having a large group of people howling at the moon several nights in a row.

Amenities

It's also important to find a place that has a hot tub or at least has room for a hot tub. People on vacation looking at vacation rentals seem to love hot tubs or pools (community or otherwise) and I would guess that it's been the difference maker for me on many dozens of occasions.

If you own a cabin or beach house sometimes having a fireplace can be kind of a big deal. There really is nothing more charming than having a fireplace in your property and although firewood is messier and possibly expensive it really can add a lot of character to a place. I have to believe that my fireplace is as large an attractant as my hot tub.

A barbeque grill is also a very nice amenity to have. A home cooked steak on the grill is usually just as good or better than ordering a steak at a restaurant only it's about 15-45 dollars cheaper per person depending on what kind of a restaurant that you are going to. The more complete your kitchen is the more that your guests can and will choose to eat at home.

Eating a few meals at home can save vacationers hundreds of dollars on their vacation suddenly making your property even more so of a bargain over a hotel where clearly you aren't going to be eating very many meals in your room. And if a hotel offers room service, well I don't have to tell you how expensive that room service food can be after tips and charges and so forth.

Having a view isn't critical but it can be helpful and also can be a difference maker. Remember that you are competing against hundreds of vacation rentals in your area so you want to have the right place at the right price. Otherwise you might find yourself bringing in lowered rental amounts or seeing your place vacant for vast portions of the year.

Views come in all shapes and sizes, water views, mountain views, landmark views, territorial views and so forth. If you are in New York City and your view is that of another building then that is going to be what it is. But if you are out in the woods or country then choosing a property that has at the very least a territorial view can be a very good thing. When marketing your property you are going to want to have a place that can boast some nice amenities and a good view of something is always a help.

Activities

Settle into an area that has stuff going on year around. The Jersey shore is probably gangbusters in the summer but how is it in the winter? Copper Mountain Colorado probably goes off in the wintertime but can it be as busy during the summer? Vermont is lovely in the fall but what about the rest of the year? Even here locally in Washington there are few places that are busy year 'round. However, Leavenworth was very smart to ensure that they stayed relevant throughout the year. In the winter there are snow activities at nearby ski and sledding resorts, December lighting festivals and horse drawn sleigh rides. In the spring, skiing is still happening but they are also shrewd enough to host any number of art walks, wine walks and 10ks and other running events. The summer months are probably their busiest months with your typical summer vacationers but there are food events, more wine events and hundreds of activities like hiking, biking, white water rafting, kayaking... the list goes on.

36.

In the fall months things can slow down a little bit as the kids head back to school and the parents head back to reality, however the Leavenworth chamber once again, in a moment of brilliance and being a "Bavarian" town have Oktoberfest weekends that go off each weekend in October. Being able to sell a weekend in October is like taking candy from a baby.

There are beer gardens and beer tents and beer tastings and woman dressed up like Saint Pauli girls and sausages and a host of other activities. So what could have been a very slow time of the year, in fact, turns into one of the busiest times of the year.

It might be hard to find a town or an area like this near your home town but even if you can keep your calendar booked three seasons out of the year you will be doing just fine. Later in this book we will talk about both marketing your property as well as you possibly can and pricing your property properly during the slower times of the year just so you can keep some cash flow coming in.

Proximity to your rental from your home

As it pertains to the location of your property it's important to consider just how far from your home that you would like it to be. If you already live in a resort town then it might serve you well to have a vacation rental in that same area. However, this does defeat the purpose of having a vacation rental. You already have a home in the area, so what would be the fun or the point of having another home super close to the home that you already have if you also plan to use it as a retreat for yourself. I think there is a fine line between having a property that is so close that you don't really feel like you've gotten away from things or so far away that it's a drag trying to get there.

I also don't think that you want a place that you have to take a plane ride to. That becomes very expensive and extremely cumbersome and of course might also involve having to rent a car and all of the other hoops that you have to jump through when you go on vacation.

I think that those types of vacations are great, however, in those situations I think that it's best to try to rent somebody else's vacation rental (and even more awesome if you can work out a trade with that vacation property owner in exchange for a stay in your own place).

Managing a cabin from a plane ride away is also very challenging, especially when it comes down to a point when you really need to be at your property, for example when my cabin was robbed in 2008. Being robbed is a very helpless feeling and even more so if you cannot be there to deal with what is happening, whether that be with insurance people, the police, replacing the stolen items at the lowest price possible and so forth.

So what is the right distance then? In my opinion a place that is an hour or an hour and a half to two or at most three hours driving distance. Four hours and that ride is going to get old after a while and you will find yourself using your property less and less. My cabin is two and a half hours away and it's very scenic through the majority of that drive (then again every drive in Washington State is pretty scenic). I never get tired of that feeling when I've driven through the last major town on my route and really start heading up into the mountains. When I arrive at the top of the pass (Steven's pass to be exact) I know that I'm only 40 minutes away and getting close. As I make the last few winding turns through the mountains with a wild raging river on my right I really start getting excited. Also being in a completely different climate is something that has its own benefits as well.

38.

Close to town or far out of town?

Another important attribute is finding a place that is near the action. That's not to say that being far out and remote might not serve you well but if there is a big town where everything happens then you are going to want to be within reasonable driving distance of that location. A good rule of thumb would be less than 10 miles. Another good rule of thumb is to perhaps not also be immediately in the thick of things either. You do want to differentiate yourself from the string of hotels that make up most tourist destinations. People rent cabins and houses to gain a bit of privacy while still being close enough to everything and so that every trip into town doesn't become some kind of event. People on vacation also like to drink and therefore want to have a place that is close enough to the bars and restaurants that they could cab home without having to spend an small fortune to do it. My cabin happens to be about 7 or so miles from town and that fortunately has worked out very well for me. Places in town can also do pretty well I'm sure especially in certain areas like Vegas (although I would pretty much recommend that Vegas might be the worst place to do a vacation rental due to the enormous amount of hotel rooms, comps, massive discounting and the severe amount of drinking and partying that goes on there). I still contend that being a short distance is the better way to go.

It's also helpful to be near points of interest if you can. An example of this for myself is that although I'm not right in town I am near a winery and a horse stable where folks can go on sleigh rides and horseback riding tours. In San Diego if you aren't in the heart of downtown you might want to look for a place near the beaches of La Jolla or the Torrey Pines Golf Course. The list goes on but being in the proximity of activities can add to the purchase price but still put you in a prime area where you can get a lot of rentals.

Weather and Climate

Another thing to consider is weather. I again am very fortunate to have a place where the weather is night and day from Seattle which also happens to be a major population area, one in which people grow very weary of cold, dark and wet days for months on end. On many days you can drive some two and a half hours and find yourself leaving cloudy, rainy cool climates and finding warm, dry and sunny climates.

If you have the good fortune to be able to do this where you live geographically then that could be a great thing also. Phoenix Arizona for example is very hot but two hours north in Sedona it can be very temperate and a great place for a family to get a quick getaway out of the heat without the hassles of the airport.   Las Vegas is ridiculously hot in the summertime but Mt. Charleston nearby is quite a bit cooler and much prettier than the desert in my opinion. San Francisco can be cool and windy year around but drive a few hours east and you've got warm, sunny temperatures, so finding a place that has better weather than a nearby major city with a huge population center can also be a real winner. Now if that particular area is too expensive to purchase property in look for cheaper adjacent towns. Sedona for example is very expensive but there are towns nearby that aren't nearly as expensive at all. Yes it can pull you out of the action a little bit but it also will allow you to reduce your rents and still be profitable which also might end up being a win for the client looking to book in the area. Really it's all about thinking outside of the box and purchasing what you can afford. With the right piece of property and with good marketing of that property you can still do very well and who knows, in a few years you just might be able to afford that big, expensive place in the hot part of town.

Number of bedrooms and size thereof

One final attribute to look for is the number and size of the bedrooms. A huge advantage of a vacation rental is that several families can pitch up together to get a place big enough to accommodate everybody. If your guests were to have to get several hotel rooms it can turn out to be way more expensive than getting one, very nice rental cabin or property. Also oftentimes a big group of friends or a bachelorette party or what have you will want to find a place where they can all coexist at the same time. Families also are not very fond of putting their small children in another hotel room by themselves giving them two choices, keep the kids in the room with them and have no privacy or put them in a strange room or maybe even an adjoining room but even then there is still that feeling that you lose a little bit of control over them and a little bit of privacy. So being all contained in the same home or property can be both less expensive and provide greater proximity and better supervision of children and it's truly a real win/win. Some hotels do now offer private residences on their properties (The Turtle Bay Hotel on the North Shore of Hawaii comes to mind or The Hana Maui Ranch) but they are incredibly expensive and usually smaller.

Now that you've located your property

Ok so you finally spotted the perfect location. What's next? Well it's time to put in your offer and hopefully in this current real estate environment you are getting a good deal. Make sure you have a real estate agent who knows what he's doing and is an expert in finding vacation rental properties.

Make sure that you have somebody who has your back and it's probably a good idea to not hire the agent who is listing the property. Make sure that you've gone down your list of things that are both important to you and important to be successful and you've met all of your requirements.

The cosmetic fixer

Now one thing that I would look for that others might not is a bit of a cosmetic fixer upper. Sometimes there are great homes that have a unique look but that seemingly need quite a bit of work, or they are a bit dated or there is a fair amount of junk lying around the property or the furnishings, which are leaving soon anyway give the place a musty dated look. These homes can sometimes stay on the market for a long time and end up getting reduced and reduced again in price. These can be real bargains.

When I bought my place it needed a lot of work but nothing too dramatic. Nothing structural, I didn't have to replace any appliances (not right away anyway) but I did have to do a lot of painting, cleaning, window washing and scrubbing. I had to take a drill and a box of screws and re-secure a lot of the wood on the deck and railings and most expensive of all I had to put in a driveway. All of the things that hadn't been done made the property look very unappealing. However, based on comps at the time, they did list their property within a range that made the property inexpensive based on those metrics. At the end of the day the cabin had a lot of nice attributes but it also had a lot of things wrong with it. I do not have a time machine but I often wonder what my cabin would have sold for during that time considering all that I've now done to it. My guess is about $100,000 more and probably wouldn't have lasted 10 days on the market.

Finding a place with this kind of potential can be a real find. Cosmetic fixers, once fixed can see a huge spike in their value but beyond that when the name of the game is cash flow doing all the right fixes can dramatically increase the nightly rate that you can charge.

Once I had purchased my cabin I had several weeks to purchase everything that I needed to buy for the cabin. I pretty much went from store to store making all of my purchases and it seemed that every day large assortments of boxes were arriving on my doorstep from all of the various companies.

The first weekend that I was actually in possession of my property I took two days off of work, called a friend and headed out to the cabin with a truckload of both new and previously owned possessions with the intention of getting my cabin entirely put together in those four days.

We worked steadily from sunup to well past sundown (60 hours in four days!) in an attempt to clean and paint and move in and landscape and then get rid of all of the endless array of boxes and trash that we had accumulated. It was insane but we got it mostly done. I also knew that I had the next several weekends to finish all of the other projects and it took each and every one of them to get everything done but once it was finished the changes were dramatic. The place had really taken shape and had my unique signature on everything. I was very proud for what I had accomplished in that month of weekends and had my place all ready to go for my first booking minus the hot tub and the driveway both of which I knew were coming. From that point till now it still is and will remain a work in progress. I have just installed a brand new deck, will be repainting the exterior of the cabin for the second time and have just purchased all new appliances. But the way I see it it's like forced savings and I'm adding to the value of my home which is both going to allow me to see the property rise in value over time and attain much higher rental income in the future.

Although I live in a fantasy world where I believe that one day all the work will be done I'm smart enough to truly understand that that will never be the case, there will always be something to do!

<u>What do clients want</u>

What are clients and potential guests looking for? Based on my experience they are looking for clean, modern and well appointed. They are willing to pay extra for the little luxuries. When they walk through the door they are going to be looking for things to be orderly, just as if they were to walk through the doors of a Hyatt or the W hotel. People again don't typically need *but are willing* to pay extra for a hot-tub, fireplace, nice furnishings and a look that suggests that you took some time and effort to make things nice. Later in this chapter I'm going to tell you all about getting your place all decked out for as little as possible.

My number one guest comment is "we loved the décor." The thing that I've truly done is I've created a home, a second home that I rent to guests when I do not have the time or ability to be there. The place is nicely appointed, warm and feels like home. People will not pay good money for cold and stark and sterile and cheap.

Now, when you spend the night in a hotel on business, or if you are grabbing a hotel near the airport so that you don't have to wake up at 4 am to drive two hours to the terminal or if you simply do not have a lot of money there is nothing wrong with a red roof inn or a motel 6 or a Rodeway Inn. It's a room with a shower and a bed and a TV. The colors are usually terrible, the materials are usually cheap and flimsy, and every single element of the room you can tell was done by the lowest possible bidder using the absolute cheapest materials. And at the end of the day this is fine. But to stay in a place like that on vacation, well to me that would be unconscionable.

44.

I mean if you are in you teens or twenties you are just so excited to be out of the house and spending the night in a place that you paid for that none of that fancy stuff really matters. You don't have a lot of money and you simply want a place where you can drink beer with your friends and after all you are never going to be there but to shower, pre-funk and sleep, if that. However, when you get older, when you have a family you are going to want to stay in a place that you can really enjoy, a place that you yourself wish that you could own but for whatever reason can't and you are going to be willing to spend the money to make it happen.

Lastly, there is so much of that inventory in popular vacation destination so why would you want to try to compete with that? You are just a small fish in a very large pond at that point. You have to set yourself apart, you have to bring something to the table that nobody else does.

There is a huge demand for this kind of property and there are those willing to pay the price to stay there. I know there are a lot of ways to go but I'm convinced that pound for pound and dollar for dollar there is no better approach to the vacation rental market.

What they don't want

What people don't want is a haphazard array of lousy furniture scattered about, a 19 inch television from 1993 and velvet bull fighter paintings. They don't want dirty windows, broken cabinets or a look that says "I'm trying to make as much money as possible off of you while simultaneously putting forth as little of my own money and effort as possible."

45.

Here's an example of this. For the last many years a group of friends and I stay at this group of condominiums on Lake Chelan called Wapato Point. We stay in different units of this individually owned condo development every year owned by different people who of course charge different rates and who have different tastes.

For many years it seemed that maybe we paid a little more and ended up in places that were pretty nice. Places where it seemed that there was that sense of pride of ownership. Beyond the interiors of these condos, however, is this very nice setting. The condos are right on the water, have their own little beach are about 10 minutes to town and are generally a good launching pad for all of the activities that we do while we are out there.

After years of success renting at Wapato the last time we stayed, being last minute and desperate, we just booked a place. The pictures that we saw online made the place just seem very generic. We were, for lack of something better and also on a time constraint, fine with generic . However, as we walked through the door the place was in obvious disrepair. The low price that we had paid quickly translated into why we paid so little. The inside smelled and looked like a college dorm. A lot of unpainted oak furniture, an old TV with no reception and no cable, a fold out couch that was in such bad shape that we just took the mattress out of the fold-out couch and laid it on the floor, which was equally scary because of how rough of shape the carpet looked like it was in. Everything was stark and white and cheap. And this led me to one feeling and one feeling only. I was glad that I had done what I had done to my place and I was convinced that when you provide clients with a place that looks like a college dorm room then people are going to treat it like a college dorm room when the resident assistant is away.

Keep in mind we treated it respectfully but it was our guess that those who stayed both prior to us and after us probably didn't show it the same level of kindness.

<u>How to deck your place out inexpensively</u>

So that said you might be thinking. "I don't have the budget to spend a bunch of money on expensive furnishings." Well the good news is that you don't have to for I am now going to provide you with the very best ways to furnish your rental property. Below is a list of where I bought everything and then a few suggestions where you might find things for even cheaper than what I had paid for them.

Your own home - The first place to look for many, many items for your new rental cabin is your own home. It's the number one source for used furnishings that clearly are going to be nice (after all you picked them out for yourself at one point) and of course once you decide to use these items for your rental you then get to go out and buy new stuff for your home. It's a nice trade-off.

Target - A great place to purchase so many things, in my opinion, at highly discounted or at very fair prices. At Target I bought DVR's, towels, duvets, a few knick-knacks, some kitchen items and housewares. Target is not going to be a great place for everything that you need but it will have a lot of the basics.

Wal Mart – At this tiny little hometown store (you may have heard of them and their charming little retail outlets) I bought a couple of Vizio flat screens, I bought all my dishware and glasses, I purchased some cookware, a microwave and a host of other items. I will say this I would never buy clothes at Wal-Mart but beyond that Wal Mart has a many of the brand name products we use every day at rock bottom prices. However, if a sense of morality prevents you from shopping here then please refer back to my Target recommendation.

47.

Overstock.com – At Overstock I purchased all my pillows, down comforters, flannel sheets and other bedding items. I saved a bundle, maybe over 70% off. (I also bought some stuff on E-bay that was barely used. Blankets and sheets and so forth get used and washed and used and washed. If you can find some items on e-bay that have been slightly used and are completely serviceable and of a good quality and attractive, buy them.)

Mattress outlets – When I bought my cabin I was lucky to hit one of those clearance sales of mix and match mattresses. I also was smart to only buy beds that required the top mattress therefore alleviating the need to even have to buy box-springs. The mattresses were comfortable as heck and I bought four of them for around $1,100. Now I probably could have gotten them cheaper at a few other places but I think that the one thing that is super important is mattress quality. If people do not sleep comfortably they will remember that and never stay again. The return on investment with a good mattress is huge. Another tip, remember to buy the plastic covers for them that go under the sheets, it will keep them like new forever, although plastic or rubber underneath they usually have a cotton or terrycloth top to them so the sheets don't slide around.

Tip #2, always buy a firm mattress, first, they are cheaper and second folks who prefer pillow top can survive on a firm mattress but somebody who needs a firm mattress for back support will suffer trying to sleep on a pillow top

Furniture Outlets – In every midsized town there is a furniture outlet. The one nearest me is called the Northwest Design Gallery. They buy mass produced, but nice, furniture and sell it with a razor thin profit margin and make up the difference through volume they also purchase furniture from China and Thailand and sell that secondhand, lastly they consign other people's used furniture in there store as well. It's very cool stuff and it is also very in touch with today's tastes.

48.

This is where I feel that I really scored. I bought a beautiful leather couch, a king bedroom set, two "Dania" style queen sized bedframes, cocktail tables and a bunch of other stuff for under $5,000. To me, that was a great deal. I would have paid twice that at a Macy's home store.

This brings me to another point; unless you have an unlimited budget, avoid the high end designer furniture galleries. Furniture really is one of those things where prices vacillate wildly. Even the same furniture from the same manufacturers can be sold at very different prices depending on a number of factors. One of the main factors is who the store caters to. Just like with clothes you can buy something at Neiman Marcus (needless markups?) for $400 or the same thing at TJ Maxx for $70. I mean if it makes you feel cool, important or catered to if you buy it at Neiman's, by all means do that, but if you want to have a dramatic impact on your rental and try to generate the most cash flow immediately then take my advice on this one. Plus with all that cash flow you will have coming in you can then actually afford to go shopping at Neiman's (but still why would you want to, myself personally, I'd rather use that money to go on vacation!) Pier One and Cost Plus are two other places that sell accent pieces, art and other cool items at relatively inexpensive prices.

If you don't have the money for the above then there are three other great places you can go to find great stuff at cheap prices; Craig's list and Amazon.com. In my opinion you could find just about everything that you need at these web sites. Craig's list, in your area, is especially great because you can, for example, find a great leather couch or flat screen TV at a super cheap price because perhaps somebody is moving. You can pick up the item locally and then pack it away for the big move-in day.

Amazon and E-bay are both great for a host of things, especially electronics, but they also require you to oftentimes pay for shipping which can cut into the deal that you've just received.

General tips for purchasing furniture for your rental

Here is a quick tip on furniture. Leather looks nice and lasts for a long time. A red wine spill on a brown leather couch (avoid suede of course) is a non-issue as it cleans right up if you take care of it quickly, do the same on a beige cloth couch and it's time to call the upholsterer or the furniture store to buy a new one.

Avoid particle board at all costs. It's cheap, it breaks and it swells in humidity and become fragile. Move it a couple of times and the connections start to degrade and eventually the "piece" of furniture will just begin to fall apart at the seams.

Buy things made of solid wood and stone and leather and so forth, things that last and which don't break easily. Hardwood flooring is a plus, area rugs from the likes of Pier One look nice and can be replaced inexpensively.

Buy nice cheap durable plates, glasses and cookware. Again Wal Mart is great. Those sturdy Mexican glasses are cheap and durable and don't often break when you drop them on the ground. The only thing I buy for my cabin that is fragile are wine glasses and trust me, I go through them, but they aren't crazy expensive and people do appreciate drinking wine from a decent glass.

Buy nice décor and don't feel bad about nailing, screwing or gluing things down. I mean not everywhere and don't glue or nail nice things to other nice things. For example in my cabin I have a very expensive old rifle hanging over the fireplace.

I have it secured to the fireplace with some metal bands and screws. Now, that is not going to stop anybody from stealing it but it might slow them down a little bit and also it keeps the gun where it belongs which is secured to the fireplace. It's from the 1800's and really doesn't need to be handled a whole bunch of times.

Also, do not have any item in the house that costs more than the security deposit that you charge. For example, I have friends that have a $20,000 telescope in their rental while charging a 500 dollar deposit. Trust in this business is everything and every time somebody walks through their door they have to cross their fingers that those guests didn't check in with a stolen credit card and a bogus security deposit check or fake credentials, so that right there is a risk that I wouldn't take!

My advice is to purchase nice things but don't have any one item that is worth a lot of money so that if that one thing is stolen you are going to really be hurt financially by it. I do have two nice TV's in my home but they were both purchased on Craig's list for very little money and if you want to risk being charged with grand theft or grand larceny for something that I paid $200 for then be my guest but I will be pressing charges if you get caught and when I give the price of that which was stolen it's not going to be the Craig's list price it's going to the full retail value. If you ever get robbed you will know exactly how I feel.

Keep your place clean, neat, simple and uncluttered. It makes doing the inventory quite easy, beyond just looking nice.

Have a place for everything. Get your rental exactly the way you like it then take pictures of it and give them to your cleaner so that when you walk through the door it's exactly the same every time.

One of the reasons that some folks like McDonalds is that they kno.. exactly what they are going to taste, smell and see whether they are in Mazatlan, Mexico or Monroe, Wisconsin. So ensure that your place looks exactly like it does in the pictures that you are using to advertise it.

Buy a nice commercial washer and dryer so that you can wash and dry sheets as quickly as possible in between guests. Any additional cost that you pay will be made up very quickly by the shorter amount of time your cleaner is going to spend washing and drying sheets. Also whether you do this right away or when your existing water heater fails purchase a commercial water heater as well. Even in a small cabin like the one that I own (1800 square feet) I still find myself receiving and accepting reservations of 8-10 people. With adults you can expect that people will all be showering up before a night out on the town, especially if they were doing activities that day. Therefore a large commercial water heater will allow all of those folks to get a hot shower, especially if they make an attempt to conserve hot water by turning off the shower while lathering up and so forth.

One very important thing to remember is to cater to your client demographic and not your own personal taste. If you are looking to attract upscale clientele or at the very least the upper middle or middle class you really need to purchase items that reflect current tastes. My best suggestion would be to get a hotel room at a W hotel or walk through an Ikea or buy a book that has plenty of photo illustrations of what it is that you are trying to achieve, whether it be beach house or cabin or metropolitan condo. Avoid any décor that caters to any one gender, you really want gender neutral décor. Floral couches and bedspreads aren't going to sit well with most men (I know people who've filed for divorce because the wife insisted on an all pink master bathroom, true story) nor would country kitchen. On the flip side of that coin most woman do not mind hanging out in a place that has a more masculine feel.

I would also add that in 2012 dark, rich color schemes are what is in vogue. Places that have that stark, white feel are nice, if you are running an operating room or interrogation room but beyond that I wouldn't go there unless you are renting out a loft in Soho or something.

The importance of being Pet Friendly

When it comes to putting your vacation rental up for rent the one thing that you do not want to do is exclude anybody. You also, on the other hand, want to be as inclusive as possible and remember one very important thing.

People with dogs typically love the outdoors and people who love the outdoors typically own dogs. People who own dogs therefore travel and most hotels simply do not accommodate pets. Therefore if you allow folks with pets to stay in your rental you are going to widen your client base dramatically.

On the VRBO system for example they have a list of things that you provide. For example, do you take credit cards, are you wheelchair accessible and do you accept pets.

Editors note: We realize that the pictures on the pages to follow are very small. This is a copy/paste editing issue and we are working on a fix. In the meantime to see any of the pictures please proceed to:

www.cabinateaglecreek.com

or

 www.vrbo.com/192335

53.

I think that the more things you can offer the better you will do. However, if you have white linen couches and 18th century furnishings - going dog friendly might not be the way to go. Also, being pet friendly may not be a huge thing in a large metropolitan city like New York. I couldn't see any conceivable reason why I would want to bring my dog to New York City with me unless if it was my girlfriend's purse dogs and even then it still is a huge hassle and you don't want to leave behind a yappy dog in an apartment complex where you know it will be annoying the neighbors and possibly causing complaints.

However, having dogs myself I knew that when I put my cabin together that I needed to ensure that everything was for the most part dog friendly. Again, leather couches, stone, wood, metal, hardwood floors, putting quilts on top of all the beds that could be washed or shook out easily, buying baby gates and so forth. This allowed me the sense that I could allow pets and be OK. I also have a stringent set of rules for pets and I charge not only a pet cleaning fee but also, of course, require a security deposit.

Security Deposits

I do find it incredibly important to make all of my guests happy and not have confrontations and let me tell you that keeping a security deposit or a portion thereof is extremely confrontational. But you have to be firm. Guests do need to read the rules and like anywhere else, being ignorant of the rules is never an excuse for breaking them.

There has been a lot of talk about the 1% lately and as it pertains to your rental you will also deal with the 1%, but this is a different 1% that I'm talking about. The 1% that I'm talking about are the 1% that will come in and treat your property poorly. There is no avoiding this. That is when you have to play hardball. I hate keeping security deposits and I've only had to do it a few times but do not hesitate to do it when things go wrong. Just because a client paid you a thousand dollars to rent your place for a long weekend does not give them carte blanche to treat your home like a flophouse. More often than not, however, the guest will know that they have screwed up and will be willing to make things right, the secret is to be fair and to charge them for the cost of the damage or extra cleaning and nothing else. There should be no "punitive damages" when charging against a client's security deposit, to me, that is unfair. Now if I'm being hit with a punitive cost from my home owners association for a large party of course I'm going to pass that along but charging a client $100 above and beyond your cleaners time as a punishment I don't think is right. It might be OK to mention the possibility of a punitive damage in your contract to help mold behavior from your guests but charging it is an altogether different thing.

I will say here, after 5 years of being pet friendly I've yet to have any serious problems due to pets. People yes, pets no. Pet owners know it's a privilege to bring their dogs with them on vacation and they seem to do all they can to follow the rules, in fact, I think they go overboard in following the rules. Pet owners in fact have been some of my best guests. My feeling is that anybody who loves their dog enough to pay extra money to bring them on vacation is going to be the kind of person that is going to care for your home as well. The couple that goes on vacation and leaves their dogs in the garage with a bowl of kibble and a bucket of water is probably not looking to rent my property either.

4

My story: How I came to manage my property on my own

When I first bought my vacation property I knew that I wanted to rent it a little bit but I, at that time, didn't really need the money and had mostly bought the place for the tax deductions and the potential for appreciation over time. To me, making those mortgage payments was like forced savings. Every mortgage payment I made created a tax deduction that reduced my taxable income which at the time, for me, was good enough. I also figured that if my place rose in value by 4-6% per year (the average annual increase of real estate over long periods of time) then I would be making some 15-25k per year from real estate appreciation alone and therefore, in essence , by doing absolutely nothing.

Of course, based on pure timing it didn't work out that way, however, that was the intention and I see things coming full circle as we speak.

Property Management firms

Out of the gate I hired a property management firm out of Leavenworth to manage my property on my behalf. This is a firm whose sole focus is to rent out cabins and lodges and other types of homes and it was my goal to make my place nice enough so that they would consider adding me to their list of properties for rent.   In the beginning I was so incredibly naïve, I simply had no clue what other options existed for myself and even if I did I would have experienced such a steep learning curve that it would have almost seemed incomprehensible to attempt running the cabin on my own. Then again I didn't have an end to end guide like you hold in your hands right now.

Interestingly enough after I had gone to closing I called this firm and asked them if they would come take a look at my property, which I had just bought and which to me was still very raw and unfinished at the time. To my surprise they told me that they had enough properties in their system and weren't really taking any more on.

Either this was the truth or a really great sales tactic that only served to make me want them more than ever! Hearing this I begged to speak to the owner and after a few moments on the phone with him he agreed to at the very least come and take a look. Luckily upon seeing the place, even in its very rough current shape, he agreed to take me on.

After I had done my vast renovation he came back around for me to sign the contract. It was at this time I would find out that they would be keeping 45% of my rental income. 45%!

Now it is true that you can make a lot more money renting by the night than you can by renting by the month but when you then have to give up almost half of that revenue to the firm that is managing it for you, well, it just then became a lot less profitable to be in the vacation rental business.

Upon hearing this I wasn't too thrilled but what choice did I have? I had no clue how to run it myself nor did I, at the time, feel that I had the resources to do it. I also felt at the time that any money that I had coming in would be better than no money coming in at all. I also knew that I wasn't, by any means, going to be spending every weekend at my cabin and to have a place sit empty for that length of time isn't doing anybody any favors.

I also found out during that meeting and contract signing that I was going to have to meet a ton of their company's standards, some of which made sense and some of which I found ridiculous. I had to, for example, buy a bunch of appliances, like blenders and an iron, that I'm pretty sure to this day haven't been used. I had to get my windows cleaned two times a year whether they needed it or not or whether I had done them or not. I had to have my driveway plowed almost every day in the winter whether it needed it or not and all of these things came out of my share of the profit, not theirs.

Later I was told that if I wanted to allow friends or family stay at my place for free, (let's say they had done me a favor and I wanted to gift the cabin to them for the weekend), I still had to pay this rental firm their share! Now to me 45% of zero is zero but not to them. They wanted 45% of what they should have been charged. This was one of the first of many moments when I thought to myself, man..... this is really starting to not make sense.

This of course only forced me to create work-arounds or put another way I just simply stopped telling them that it was a friend of mine staying in the cabin, I just told them that I would be staying there instead. They also didn't let me do the clean if I felt like saving 90 bucks, I had to let them do the clean after even I stayed there. I understand their concerns being that they are trying to create a standard and protect their image but I can assure you I am a way better cleaner than whoever they were hiring to do the job for them. I really think that this particular business was failing to remember who had paid for and renovated and was making the payments on the cabin. Now if you are an extremely busy person and you do not have time at all to manage your property then I guess that a property management company is going to be your only course of action if you need some recurring revenue but if you think you can do it on your own in your spare time you should. Nobody is going to care about how often your place gets rented out more than you are.

What is also important, I would assume, is how large your mortgage is relative to your property or if in fact you have your property paid off. If this is the case then you might be willing to accept less in the way of revenue or be more willing to share your revenue with a property manager. However, I'm not there yet and if you are reading this book I will assume that you aren't there yet either.

Sometimes we can get caught in that trap of thinking that there isn't another option and we are afraid to go a different route for fear that it's not going to work out. Again, it's that same fear that traps many people into a low or average hourly wage when they could very well become very successful in something like sales where the income potential is technically limitless.

From bad to worse

Things went on like this for probably a year or longer. I couldn't have been less happy. They rented my place out almost every day in the month of December of 2007 and I got a check in the mail for like 700 dollars, or put another way, around three days' worth of revenue. When asked why the check was so horribly low they attributed it to all the plowing that needed to be done. With that many families spending that many days during that cold of a month I'm not even certain that the check covered my heating and firewood bill. I calculated that that month the cabin brought in $4500, they kept $2,025 dollars, they sent me $700 and they paid the spa people, the plow-man and the cleaners $1,775 dollars. It was moments like this that I began dreaming of the day when I could figure out a way to run the cabin myself or find somebody else who could run things as effectively as they were but at a lower percentage.

There was one super important thing that I learned from dealing with this firm. They had no skin in the game as it pertained to costs. They were going to get their nut no matter what..... and my goals, desires and need for income was not their concern in the slightest. Additionally, I wasn't nearly a priority for them in any way, shape or form. I was nothing more than, analogy-wise, a box of cereal on a shelf with a bunch of other boxes of cereal. So even though I invented the product, and packaging and did some of the marketing and the advertising I was still at the mercy of the grocery store that was going to sell me at a 50% mark up. I had no say as to where on the shelf I would be or how hard the clerks would work to sell me over anybody else. My cabin had in fact become nothing more than a widget.

From the very beginning with this firm there was nothing but warning signs and red flags that this wasn't going to end well....the low revenue, the feeling that I was the least of their concerns or worries, the fact that the owners just always seemed overwhelmed with any number of current problems. Their receptionist, who was also in charge of handling the office and therefore the requests of the cabin or property owners, was for lack of a better term incredibly surly.

The final straw came when I needed to have an appraisal done on my place to do a very critical refinance which was going to take me from 5.75% fixed to a 5% 5/1 option arm fixed for five years (I figured if rates rose I could always refinance again). I had called and asked if somebody from the firm could go out and let the appraiser in and the firm agreed that they would do that for me. "Great I thought, finally, they are doing something to help me out." This of course was after a series of strenuous conversations about everything else that I felt that they weren't doing very well. So I felt glad for a moment that they were going to step up and lend me a hand.

When the day came for the appraisal to be done I called the firm to remind them of the obligation and their promise to help me out. I didn't get a hold of the" powers that be" but I was able to leave a message for the owner with their "receptionist/ office manager".

When the time came for the appraisal, (mind you the appraiser was driving some 100 plus miles one way to do the appraisal), nobody from the firm was to be found to let the guy in. So after waiting around outside for a period of time the appraiser of course left and I had, once again, been shafted by them.

That turned out to be the final straw for me. At this point I realized that even if I simply just took the place off the rental market, in relation to the money that I was bringing in from the company, that I would find a way to be OK. I'd make the payment somehow and I certainly would have a lot less wear and tear on the cabin. There just comes that point when you as a renter realize that it just isn't worth it to pay somebody to do something that you should probably learn to do yourself.

I was fortunate that I had absolute proof that they had let me down which in a way kind of put them into a breach of contract type of a situation. I mean technically they were in the process of doing me a favor and then fell very short of following through. But based on all of the other problems that I had had with them when I called the owner to tell him that I wanted out of their system he basically told me that he would release me from the contract, (the contract that I had signed also had a time constraint added to the language that I would use them and only them for a period of time.) Saying goodbye to them was scary, pretty much on par with quitting your job as a restaurant manager to open up a new restaurant across the street but knowing in your heart that you can do a better job and knowing that in time, with hard work, that everything will work out.

Hiring a new manager

But before I was ready for that large of a leap I called around to see if I could find somebody else to yet manage it for me.

Of course I immediately began looking for a better plan B and after calling around for a bit and asking around town for a referral I did find a woman who was interested in managing my cabin.

63.

She only took 20% which was already quite a better deal and so I immediately hired her.

So much of this business is based on trust but in my particular case it was also based on desperation. Sometimes you want to believe that somebody is more qualified than they really are just so that you can quickly delegate the management and move on. This typically turns out to be a bad idea.

After bringing this new gal onboard things did go pretty well for a while. The fact of the matter remained in this case that she had cabins of her own and you can bet your last dime that she would be renting hers first and mine as an afterthought, but she had enough business that I was a benefactor of what can only be described as "trickle-down economics". When folks would call to rent my cabin or her cabin and hers was booked then and only then would she book mine. If somebody called to rent my cabin, if she couldn't steer the client back towards hers then I would end up with the booking. (I had several guests who worked to find my cabin again after I moved on from her who corroborated this).

But again I probably had doubled what I was making with the previous firm so that was still a good thing. Of course when you are on a crash course with destiny sooner or later something is going to upset the system.

It wasn't but 7 or so months into our relationship when I would have my property broken into for the first time. This is the sad fact of rental properties. They sit alone with nobody in them for days at a time and sooner or later somebody gets it into their head to come and rob you blind. And let me tell you, being robbed is a very helpless feeling made even more helpless by the fact that you are several hundred miles away from your rental property.

Being robbed for the first time

At the time that I had been robbed I had a security system that came with the house when I bought it but I never bothered to ever activate it. I just didn't think that it was going to be necessary. Leavenworth is such a wholesome town. Also, I had just gone a full year security problem free and I just really felt that Leavenworth is such a salt of the earth community that it just wouldn't happen to me. But of course I failed to forget that in these gorgeous little mountain towns that there is a serious case of the "haves" and the "have nots". There are the business owners and the second home owners and the vacationers and then there are those that toil for minimum wage serving these folks. Then in a bad economy, like in 2008, you have those who might suddenly find themselves unemployed and trying to find a way to feed their family, or worse, an addiction.

I will never know the true story of what happened but the end result of this robbery was that they got me for two flat screen TVs, DVD players, a pressure sprayer and a few nick naks. I had spent some 800 dollars for those two TVs but to me it wasn't how much they took but how much it was going to cost me to replace everything.

I was savvy enough to take a very nice "picture tube" TV from my house and put that in the bedroom, which really for a rental cabin is good enough; if you are in the middle of heaven on earth and you want to spend your time in front of a TV well then I would question that. Even if you are on crutches you can still stare out at a sunset or something. That said I did go and by buy another 31" Vizio from Wal-Mart which was on sale and an "open box" buy taboot so it was pretty darn cheap. So out the door it was a total loss of around $290 dollars, yet another benefit of being resourceful.

65.

Additionally I knew that they would never steal that ginormous TV in the bedroom as it weighs a hundred pounds and has a street value of minus twenty dollars. People really just do not want big old tube TV's anymore.

In the aftermath of the robbery I went back to the property manager that I had hired to run my property for me to try to figure out what had gone wrong. Clearly somebody had made a mistake somewhere, perhaps a door hadn't been locked or a cleaner had left a window open but nonetheless I was trying to find a way so that we could, ever so partially, all take a part in the loss and move forward. I mean I know for a fact that I wasn't involved in the theft. The guest had checked out successfully, the cabin had been robbed during the middle of the week. Clearly there had been an error on the part of the property manager or the cleaner who she had hired. I didn't want to start pointing fingers or laying down accusations. I just wanted to quickly move past this issue with everybody agreeing to be ever so slightly culpable and responsible in getting the place whole again.

All that I had asked was that she forgo a portion of her profits on the next guest that checked in. I also asked that perhaps the cleaner give me one free clean, a few hours of their time just to help a guy out. Just in case they had been the ones that had made the mistake. However, upon mentioning this to my current property manager she became very offended. With all of my efforts to not point fingers she basically said that for her to pitch in anything would be as if she were admitting fault and this was not a woman that admitted fault very easily. In fact she became very defensive and a little bit mean and it was at this point where I decided that I didn't want to work with this woman anymore. I had also learned that if you look hard enough you can absolutely find somebody else to do the job. So at this point I basically told her that our relationship was over and that I would be looking to hire somebody else.

66.

So this woman in refusing to give up $100 in payout ended up losing out on thousands and thousands of dollars in potential future revenue. Not only did this separation teach me a lot about not working with people that you don't care for but it also taught me about the importance of picking and choosing your battles wisely with guests. You do not, after all, want to lose a great guest that could mean thousands of dollars to you in future rentals or referrals over a broken wine glass or something frivolous like that.

In the aftermath of this robbery I merely took the step of finally activating the alarm system that already came with the home, something that I should have done a long time ago. Sadly, it would soon prove to not be nearly enough. The problem with keys is that once somebody is in possession of them they can very easily go and have another set made. Upon doing that all they have to do next is merely wait a few weeks or a few months come back to the property and walk right through the front door. If the guest that has just checked out has forgotten to set the alarm then that person is going to have carte blanche to take his sweet time robbing you. They might even be so kind as to lock the door on their way out. With literally hundreds of fingerprints all over the cabin there is no way that anybody is going to be dusting for prints, not to mention that the robbers prints might very well be there from the time that they last stayed. In essence giving somebody a key to your place is like giving them a hall pass to rob you in the future.

<u>An aside on securing your property</u>

Finally after having been robbed the second time I wised up and went security crazy. I went out and purchased a Schlage key pad lock system (instead of using keys you provide guests with a new passcode for each stay. (the passcode that we create is based on an algorithm that I can pretty much do in my head and it involves mixing up the day and month of the year that the client is checking in.) I also purchased a surveillance camera system just in case that the thefts were (at the time) possibly related to some elaborate inside job. Of course everything that I have done security wise is still merely a deterrent. People could still break a window, tolerate the screeching, loud alarm and wear ski masks to avoid detection but again, all that risk and potential jail time for a 300 dollar flat screen television is probably not very likely and beyond that since I've installed these systems I haven't had so much as a wash cloth go walking off.

In conclusion you need to install an alarm, you should absolutely have a keypad lock instead of providing guests with keys and you also should consider surveillance cameras. The trick there is to either have them outside (waterproof outdoor system) or if you have cameras inside make sure that they are only pointing out towards the entry or any other doors. My cameras inside the cabin only record to a DVR in the cabin and only store information for about two weeks. If I were to be robbed I would review the film for details but that is the only time that I would be seeing that and I let clients know that in my contract. I've only had one time where somebody didn't want to stay at the cabin because of the cameras and that is fine, who knows what their motivations were but I found another renter anyway.

And you will also find that if you ever do get robbed it's not so much the things they take so much as it's the act of being violated in that regard. The fact that some rogue person broke into your home and ran off with your possessions. That is the thing that gets you.

As far as things that you might leave outside like a snow blower, pressure sprayer or anything else of value it's my suggestion that you chain and lock all of those things up as well. There is a good chance that if you have a rental that some thief out there knows about it and has already cased your place. If they know they aren't going to get much without a huge hassle they will usually go and rob somebody else.

Lastly, although I haven't done this yet it might also serve you well to lock up your hot tub when you aren't there. There are locking hot tub straps and yes they aren't foolproof at all however they are a deterrent to late night drunken kids enjoying a nice hot tub at your expense.

Property manager number three

Having dealt with the theft I went searching again for another property manager and finally found one a few days later. Now this gal would turn out to be unwittingly critical in helping me to figure the next big step in how to manage the place for myself as she introduced me to the amazing world of VRBO or Vacation Rental by Owner.

Upon hiring this new person I asked her what her plan was going to be to manage my property and to market it to the masses and that is when she told me about this online system for matching renters with property owners. I was, of course, skeptical. I just couldn't imagine that a single, global website could bring in enough traffic to effectively keep your vacation property booked out (although why I felt this I don't know considering that the first firm I hired had their own proprietary website for renting out their properties only.)

But lo and behold almost immediately she started to fill up my calendar with bookings. She was also only taking 20% and she also was kind enough to let me borrow a few other important items like her contract, (which of course makes each rental legal and binding and which of course both protects you and the renter) and her arrival letter, which instructs clients on how to function at your cabin or unit while they are there. It's also a sort of "rules of the road" and a list of do's and don'ts that really might not be beneficial to the guest if it were buried in the small print of your contract. (Not that anything hidden in the fine print is really beneficial when you are trying to run a legitimate business.)

Taking the cabin over and running it myself

I really think that it wasn't a few months after watching her do this that I realized that I could most likely run the property by myself but I wasn't really sure at that point if I wanted to, however around that time, as fate would have it we ended up with a double booking. Making matters worse was the fact that I was on a one month vacation in Brazil. (during the height of the financial collapse making the trip super enjoyable) Therefore I was relying on her more than ever to manage my property in my absence. Double bookings are the bane of the vacation rental industry and will prove to create drama filled days, or at best, hours for you.

There are a lot of bad things that can happen to your vacation rental; in order they are probably fire, flood, theft and having a double booking. I will cover how to overcome these in my troubleshooting guide. That said, due to the double booking the client was offered an opportunity to stay at my property manager's cabin, which was a tad inferior to my own and additionally she just really handled the customer service end of this situation not as well as would have been preferred,

70.

leaving myself in a situation where I had a very irritated former guest and a sizeable loss of revenue.

After all of the problems, costs, dropped balls and irresponsible acts committed by this trio of property managers (though they did get progressively better) I just knew that one way or another that I was going to have to run the place myself because nobody is going to take the time to do the job right like you will when you choose to do it yourself. So after the double booking debacle, my most recent property manager too came to realize that for the amount of time she was putting in, the 20% of the revenue that she was collecting (basically $100 or so per booking) was simply not enough to deal with the stress and aggravation that comes with dealing with guests, cleaners, contracts, inquiries, negotiations, etc. Plus she had a full time job and was running her own cabin and was both a wife and mother to her family, therefore we pretty much agreed to part ways as friends. In doing so she got her life back but she also handed me the very basic blueprint of how I could run the cabin by myself. Of course over the years that followed I went about streamlining and improving upon every single element of my property and the management thereof.

Finally at this stage I knew how VRBO worked. I had a website, a contract, an arrival letter and I knew that even if I had to take it slow for a while that I would eventually figure things out and still be light years ahead, revenue-wise, from where I was with the original property manager. Not having to pay out $400 or as much as $800 dollars a month to somebody else to do things that you could be doing yourself is a pretty cool thing. That is how you move forward in life, you try new things and you become expert at them over time simply by doing them over and over again. But with that said, the moment that I took everything over things began to go much more smoothly and if there were any issues I now knew that I owned those issues and I would only have myself to blame, which is very empowering.

71.

I now held the keys to everything and therefore it was now time to make it my own.

And sure I still have to work at this and it's not all a bed of roses but I have far less problems today than I ever had while bringing in way more revenue.

The real estate collapse and its impact

By the time that I did take things over however we were right in the heart of an economic meltdown. People were scared to spend money not knowing what was going to happen next. When I officially took over in April of 2009 the Dow Jones Industrial Average had bottomed out at around 6400 having falling from an all-time high of 14,400 - a 52% decline.

In addition to taking over the cabin and running it myself and in addition to the stock market failing and people running for their financial lives I was also in the midst of watching my firm, one of the ten largest banks in the United States, fail.

When your company, which was once trading at $44 a share is now suddenly selling for a couple of dollars a share and when every newspaper on the planet has forecasted its demise, that can be a very scary time. But it just goes to show you how really anything is possible when you have no choice but to just simply keep moving forward. The time when many people finally find success is when failure is not an option. To this day I'm not sure if failing is a matter of bad luck or just people who simply do not have the lack of ego necessary to allow themselves to fail. To me the people that I've met who are successful are those who work very, very hard at one thing until they find success in it. I mean for me it would have been massively humiliating to lose anything that I had worked so hard to attain.

72.

This wasn't just some stick built home on a piece of dirt, this was my dream that was at stake. I had worked so hard to make it to this point, I had done so many improvements to the cabin, I had invested so much money on furnishings and so forth. If we learn anything in life it's that furnishings and household possessions are worth literally nothing second hand and especially at the height of a financial meltdown, so for me I simply had to find a way to make it through by any means necessary.

Even though the market's collapse was mostly psychological, people were feeling less rich. So the first thing that I did was reduce my pricing a bit. I ran more specials; I gave out free nights to those willing to pay full price for the weekend and tried to find ways to cater to those that hadn't been so badly impacted by the financial meltdown. There were some reasons to take heart. Microsoft, an obviously large corporation in the area, wasn't laying people off and those folks make very nice livings and also seem to travel quite a bit. I would say that one in five of my guests are Microsoft employees. I also was getting a lot of business from firemen, policemen and school teachers which by and large are recession proof careers. So the good news here was that there were still some people travelling and there were pockets of the economy that, by and large, were left relatively unaffected. So my job was to go after these folks.

I also went after the "stay-cationers", folks that were planning on setting up a tent in the backyard as opposed to flying the whole family to Hawaii. With some of the discounts and promotions that I was running I was able to lure some of those people out to my cabin instead. One of the great things about a rental cabin with a full kitchen again is that a family on a budget can make all of their meals at home saving them perhaps hundreds of dollars, additionally being able to drive to their vacation means not having to get a rental car either saving them perhaps hundreds more.

73.

With me throwing in a free day or sometimes even two free days (knowing I wouldn't get the weekdays booked most likely anyway) I was able to make it worth their time and money to come and stay. Leavenworth, also has a ton of free stuff to do (hiking, biking, swimming in the rivers and lakes, bon fires, hot tubbing, star gazing, the list goes on) enabling them to feel financially secure taking the vacation while also getting their kids out of the neighborhood for a few days.

Even being lower middle class as I was growing up if my parents told me that our vacation for the year was going to be camping out in the back yard I would have probably ran to my room with a stream of hot tears coming down my face, but I digress......

At the time that I took over we were also in the heart of spring, which for me is also one of the slowest rental periods of the year in Leavenworth and wherever your property is located you are going to quickly figure out what your slow times of the year are going to be as well. But even though I was taking this double hit of struggling through a great recession and dealing with the typical spring slowdown, by reducing my pricing and running the right specials I was able to stay fairly busy and at the very least keep my place rented on the weekends and at the very, very least I was able to make my mortgage payment.

I remember sitting down at that time and looking at my total income from work and from the cabin and then also looking at this big stack of bills in front of me and thinking to myself, how in the world am I going to make this work? So I would just simply pay what I could, I made minimum payments on my credit cards; I also sacrificed all of the little luxuries of life. For about a good year I didn't eat out, didn't buy new clothes, I remember needing two new tires for my car and ending up buying a set of tires on eBay that had like 80% tread left for a fifth what I would have paid for new tires, in fact at one point each one of the tires on my car was from a different manufacturer. I also fixed things myself instead of buying new things.

74.

I got rid of my landscaper and housecleaner and started doing it all on my own.

Little by little I found myself working my way through. The summer arrived, cabin revenue began picking up, the stock market starting coming back to life and things were getting slightly better for me at my regular job, people were still panicked but thank goodness for the clients that I had in my financial advisory practice who chose to stay the course and even better than that were those who took my investment advice and who became more aggressive in the Spring of '09.

 At that point I honestly felt that either the market would come all the way back over time or that it was going to go to zero and that life as we knew it was going to become a thing of the past and therefore it wouldn't really matter a whole heck of a lot. For those of you who might be reading this in the future and who may have forgotten just how bad things got I cannot tell you how many of my clients were cashing out their meager investments to purchase guns, bullets, whiskey, cigarettes, gold bullion and anything else that could have been traded for the types of goods that keep people alive during these pre Armageddon types of moments. It was starting to feel like post World War II Germany or something.

 The thing that I also felt was that I was getting an education in proprietorship, advertising, marketing and most importantly, how to survive in business when the chips are down and the odds are stacked against you. I knew at that time that if I could make it through this I could make it through just about anything and when you have this attitude you are going to fare far better over the long run because as we've learned nothing, good or bad, ever lasts forever.

 In conclusion, beginning to rent my place out by myself during this terrible time was almost like a baptism by fire.

If I could begin the process of running my property by myself during this awful period in our financial history - just think of how much easier it's going to be for you.

Therefore I honestly believe that if you can adhere to the lessons put forth in this book and if you can begin managing your property while not in the midst of a financial crisis then you can do even better than I did.

As I conclude this chapter one of the most important things you will ever do upon taking over the management of your property will be to hire one really great person to run your property for you in your absence. Instead of having a property manager and a cleaner it's so much better to hire an independent contractor to clean your cabin while also dealing with door codes, alarm codes, restocking of supplies and any concierge work that comes along. And that leads me to my last section of this chapter which is……

Tips on Hiring good staff

One of the greatest challenges that you will face will be to hire somebody to take care of your cabin in your absence.

If you have a property in a small town which is most often times the case but not always, it is sometimes not going to be easy to find staff. Usually in a town with a bunch of vacation rentals there are going to be firms that solicit themselves as "be all end all" servicers of vacation rentals. You are probably also going to find a handful of companies that service hot tubs and also probably plow companies if you have a property in an area where snowfall is prevalent.

The thing that I've found is that these companies can sometimes leave a lot to be desired. Oftentimes they take on more clients than they can handle and end up disappointing you at one point or another, usually at the worst time possible.

During the summer months the plow companies sign up a lot of new clients, they usually over commit in an effort to keep themselves booked and busy during the winter months. Then when all hell breaks loose with a big snowstorm they've got more than they can handle - especially when the snow is coming down so hard that properties need to be done multiple times in a day. If you are getting dumped on, say a couple of feet of snow in a 12 hour period, then having the first 6 inches of snow removed isn't going to help the client get through the next foot and a half that fell but was unattended to. Sure the guys or gals came out and took care of you once but tell the client that now all they have to do is make it down the driveway through the other 18 inches. They are not going to be pleased.

Therefore the thing that you have to do is really look around. Word of mouth is the very best way to accomplish your goal of hiring staff that you can count on. I'm not saying the big service companies are bad, I'm just saying that if you can find somebody who maybe operates a little bit more independently, if you can hire an individual as opposed to a company you might find that you are getting more individualized service.

I also think that you might find that it's going to be less expensive. With a larger company they are going to have a lot of additional overhead. You might have an owner and management and they might have a lease payment and then payroll. All that overhead starts to add up and as it does so will their fees.

Background checks

When hiring somebody, make sure to do a background check, it could be the best $45 dollars that you might ever spend. If it turns out the person has ever committed a crime of moral turpitude (i.e. theft),

77.

drugs or violence related in the last couple of years you may wish to take that into consideration. I am a strong believer, however, that people sometimes deserve a second chance - especially if their infraction was many years in the past.

I will say though that prior theft convictions are especially troubling as are prior drug convictions. I had the misfortune of hiring a cleaner at one point early on who had fallen back into a pretty serious substance abuse problem. Suddenly I was getting a lot of complaints that my rental wasn't very clean and then she started to make mistakes with her schedule where she would not show up at all when the cleanings were scheduled to take place. There also was a suddenly high amount of finger pointing. Whenever the place was left clean she claimed to have done it. Whenever there was a complaint she would tell me that it was her employee or underling who had done the poor job. I would come to find out later that it was just the opposite. When I would bring these complaints to her attention she wouldn't believe me so I would have to forward the email from the guest and upon receiving it she would say, "I don't know what these people expect from me!". It was really tough but finally she made all of our lives much easier by simply quitting.

Which leads to my next story, when you are an absentee owner and your sole cleaner quits it is going to throw you into a tailspin. You now, depending on when your next check in is, have anywhere from a few days to a week or so at most to hire somebody else. Therefore it's always good to have somebody on the backburner or to create relationships with some of these larger cleaning or home maintenance firms to be able to use until you can find a permanent replacement. Therefore if you choose to manage your own property you are not only going to need to hire one person but you should also immediately line up a back-up person as well.

When this happened to me I called everybody I knew to include the local real estate office, my old rental management company (who views me as the competition and really wasn't too interested in helping) a local day spa, etc. etc. And luckily within a few hours I was referred to someone willing to take up the job. Fortunately he worked out really well and he was able to start right away and I had no hiccups in the day to day operations of my business but I also feel that I got very lucky. Eventually he moved on and I was able to find someone else who still works for me and is doing a great job as well. It's really the luck of the draw.

If you do find a great cleaner that you can trust and who takes care of all of your property's responsibilities (especially if you can get them to agree to take on your hot tub and plowing responsibilities as well) then you are going to want to treat that person extremely well. Pay them well. We currently charge $129 dollars for the clean and I let my cleaner keep the whole thing. She handles the cleaning, door codes, in town emergency situations (lock outs, etc.) and the hot tub. She does a great job and works whenever I need her without complaint or requests for days off. In short she is amazing.

If your property is running well, depending on its size you should be generating anywhere from $2,400-$5,000 or more per month, if your cleaner is working 12 or even 18 hours a month you are talking about paying out $400-$800 per month. Considering that the cleaning fees in the vacation rental business are above and beyond the price per day to stay there you really aren't missing out on anything.

An aside on the larger firms that provide cleaning and maintenance: I do no have any problem with these firms and in fact they just might be the route that you might want to go. Often they are bonded and insured and have a large staff of people all ready to go to do a host of great things for your property if and when you need them to be done.

The reason that I do not go that route is that when you hire a big firm that is running a bunch of properties you end up becoming merely a number. There is no personal relationship so therefore you will find that things get done on their timeline and not yours. Plus if you need anything done that is above and beyond the typical day to day stuff they are going to charge you quite a bit to get that done or not make an attempt to get it done at all. If you need a doorknob swapped out, they may refer you to a locksmith and that is going to be big bucks. If you need errands run or supplies picked up, again, if it's not a part of their normal array of services it's going to be expensive. So my suggestion is find someone to partner with in your business. Pay them well. Oftentimes my cleaner/manager will purchase my supplies while she does her family's shopping. Sometimes she will do my cabin sheets while doing her family's laundry. Ye s I still get charged but not nearly what a big firm would try to charge me. My cleaner isn't there to do me favors and I always offer to pay her for anything that she does above and beyond the call of duty but there is also that implied agreement that I'm going to take care of her and she isn't going to take advantage of me and that works out really well.

80.

5

Marketing Your Rental Property

Marketing 101

Marketing your property effectively is obviously going to be your first and most important hurdle once you have your place purchased, remodeled if necessary, furnished and ready for guests. If people do not know about your property then you are going to have a hard time renting it out.

For me, there is no better way to rent out your property than through vacation rental by owner or VRBO (found online at www.vrbo.com)

The marketing miracle that is Vacation Rental By Owner

Vacation Rental by Owner (VRBO) is, in my opinion, the only way to go when it comes to marketing your property to the masses. It is in essence to the vacation rental industry what Orbitz, Priceline and Expedia are to finding air transportation, a rental car or a hotel room. VRBO is easy to set up, easy to function within the confines of and in addition to all that I think that you will be amazed at the instantaneous amount of inquiries that you are suddenly going to be getting for your cabin if you position yourself correctly.

This book is not meant to be a technical "how to" of how to set up your VRBO account but I will give you all of the tips and pointers on how to effectively use VRBO that I've learned over the last 4 or so years since I've been running the cabin on my own. I do remember when I was tasked with setting up my vrbo.com site and feeling overwhelmed with all that it entailed. But the set-up is really step by step and fairly intuitive. If you feel that you are not a great writer or have a hard time being descriptive I imagine that you could always hire one of your writer friends to write something nice for you. The closest thing that I can think of to VRBO is Match.com. If you've ever been on Match.com and set up one of those sites then you will know exactly how to set up Vrbo.com. You simply position your cabin in the best light possible, put up some of the best pictures you've ever taken of the place and then write extremely flattering things about your property. It's just that simple.

Tips on setting up your VRBO account

<u>Photos</u>

As it pertains to setting up your VRBO account I have a few things to suggest. Number one, if you are not a good photographer or if you do not have a good camera hire somebody to come to your property and take the photos. A cameraman with a fish eye lens, a lens that although is designed to add size to a room, can serve the purpose of creating photos that show off your place in greater detail. The trick here is not to try and create a false vision of your property. In fact that is pretty self-defeating. You do not want to present your cabin one way online and then have it be something else when your guests arrive, in the same way that you don't want a picture from 15 years ago on your match.com profile or a stock photo of your car in place of a real photo of your auto on cars.com. It might serve your interests up front but will not serve your interests on the back end and 99% of the time it will backfire. I have a few fisheye lens photos on my VRBO site but only so that folks can really get a feel for some of the details of the place. The photos were taken by a professional with a professional camera. The pictures are well lit, have great picture quality and clarity and do wonders for my cabin's appearance and aesthetics.

Now VRBO used to have a system by which the more photos that you put on your site (up to a maximum of 16) the higher your entry would be for that particular area. If you had the full cache of 16 photos then you would be as high up the list as other properties with 16 photos and then it would go to a seniority system, meaning the longer that you were on vrbo the higher you would be. The good news here is that the higher up you are the more quickly you are going to be seen. If there is an eye catching cabin at the right price and the renter sees that photo before they come to yours then you might not ever even have a chance to sell that renter on your place. An example of this was when I was picking a place to stay when I was taking a trip to Scottsdale.

83.

There is simply so much inventory down there you are never going to be able to see it all so you end up finding a few that make sense and submitting your inquiries and hoping that somebody comes back to you fairly quickly.

Just recently, however, they changed their policy to where everybody now gets the full 16 photos and how high up you are is determined by a series of price points that you are willing to pay. The more you pay the higher up you are and with 16 allowable photos I assume VRBO creates an environment where the guest gets to see the full details of the rental and doesn't end up on the receiving end of an unfortunate surprise.

The pricing ranges from around $300 per year to almost $700 per year but just an additional booking per year will pay for the difference between the best and worst positioning. I believe that being as high up as I can possibly be nets me thousands of dollars per year more than if I were way down the list.

Having the extra photos also helps to demonstrate what my cabin is bringing to the table. I have photos of every single room and each area of some of the larger rooms. I have pictures of all of my amenities like the hot tub and the fireplace while they are in action. I have several pictures of the outside of the cabin and the property and also what kind of views that they can expect. I think it's also important to be cognizant of your surroundings when taking the photos. Most every area is going to have a sore spot. Maybe it's a nearby property that is in poor condition, or a large dead tree on the property next door. Be careful to frame your photos so that it reflects your property in the best way possible and avoids some of the eyesores that may exist in the area. However, the main thing is to be as truthful as possible. If you property is next to an abandoned or foreclosed home you don't want to take a picture of your property looking through the property next door but you may wish to frame it in the background and then let your guests know what they may catch a glimpse of.

What are some red flags that would make me nervous about renting a place? Things like merely posting a few pictures of the inside or a place that advertises itself as a three bedroom but has a picture of only one bedroom, not having pictures of the outside, pictures of the surrounding area, picture of the kitchen or bathroom (these have a tendency to be the most expensive to update therefore they have a tendency, in older properties, to not be updated). In my opinion it's better to do the very best you can with the room that you have, updated or not and illustrate those properly than to be tricky and simply not show those sore spots in your property.

Setting up an account

VRBO is very simple to get started with. There is a step by step process that you get walked through; you are going to answer a number of questions regarding your properties amenities. Be honest and thorough. Do not over promise and under deliver. That will get you into more trouble than anything else I can think of. Be clear and concise with what your property is. When writing out your properties description, be sure to mention all of the great things that your property brings to the table, talk about what sets you apart, talk up your amenities.

It is also critical that you constantly update your VRBO site. There are busy times of the year and there are slow times of the year so be sure that you are running specials and promotions during the slow times. In a later chapter I will discuss some that have worked for me.

There is one simple field, in the description tab in the listing manager menu, where you can adjust most of your pricing and promotions, just a little tagline that can lure people in to check out your site.

People love discounts such as last minute discounts, and discounts for seniors, etc. therefore it's important to know your property, know your market, understand what the next month out is likely to bring and adjust your taglines accordingly. Do not have a static tagline year around, running promotions will garner you income during the slow months, months that you are most certainly going to have to deal with.

Right now, for example, as I'm sitting her looking out at the current month I noticed that I have a couple of weekday periods in July that I can rent. Where a lot of times the predictable weekend rentals are going to be your bread and butter the weekday rentals are going to be the icing on the cake. Booking out the weekends will get all the bills paid but it's getting the weekdays rented out that are going to provide you with the excess cash flow or in other words the disposable income.

Then, down below in the pricing section, make sure to have a base price that is low but still a price point that is going to make it worthwhile for you to do the rental. For example, my base rate, the absolute lowest that I will go, is $125 dollars a night (keeping in mind that the cost for the cleaning is above and beyond that price) I arrived at that by taking the mortgage, electric, the cost of the firewood people might use and even, in the winter, the cost of plowing into the equation and at $125 dollars a night I'm just slightly above break-even.

So at any price below that it sometimes just might make more sense to not even rent it at all so as to give the cabin a small breather and cut down on the wear and tear just a bit.

I'm also always making sure to be running at least a few recurring specials on my VRBO site.

86.

You are going to find the ones that will work for you but people do love a deal and there are some great tricks out there to generate the revenue that you are going to need *and want* while making the client feel that they are getting a good bargain in return. A few that I will discuss in a later chapter are percentage discounts for certain slow times of the year and free nights in exchange for booking several nights in a row at full price.

VRBO also has a host of other features, benefits and amenities and they continue to add to their array of products all the time. It seems that with VRBO the more amenities you sign up for the higher that you will climb in their search fields as well creating a prominent space for your rental in their system for the particular area that you are in. How high up you are could determine whether people easily come across you or not when looking for a property. It's the reason why people name their plumbing firm AAA plumbing, so that they can be at the very top of the phone book for that particular category.

One of their latest additions is "Book It Now". Book it now allows guests to book and pay right through your VRBO site. They pay with a credit card after clicking on a link and the money goes directly into your checking account. This is a nice feature and one that I've just signed up for. The only problem with this system is that pricing is always changing. Certain weekends command a premium whereas other weekends do not and there isn't any way to customize it to that level. People also like to negotiate and there also isn't a calculation for extra guest fees and other fees of that nature. Therefore the system really isn't malleable enough to make it perfect but for very basic straightforward stays it could be a decent addition.

There are a bunch of other features on VRBO that I'm currently not taking advantage of but am constantly thinking about adding.

It is to a point a kind of "a la carte" or cafeteria style system and you can pick and choose what is going to work for you. Once you have a system in place, as other amenities and features come along, you can determine whether or not they make sense for you and add them. Keep in mind as mentioned that VRBO rewards you with higher placement when you do.

Business Cards

Although business cards are not going to have a huge influence on bringing in clients you can use them effectively to help to acquire guests. One of the things that I do is leave a few business cards near my guest "log book". The business card has my logo and all necessary information (name, address, phone number, web address, etc.) but at the bottom in very tiny font it says "present this card for 10% off of your stay at the Cabin at Eagle Creek."

Best case scenario the current guest grabs a few cards and keeps one for himself and hands a few to some friends. Obviously word of mouth is going to be the best thing that you can ever have in the cabin rental business but also providing the client a discount out of the gate is potentially going to give them an impetus to come and stay at your property. I have definitely received a ton of word of mouth business but I have yet to have somebody turn in one of the business cards asking for their discount, that said the cards cost me very little and if nothing else add a bit to my sense of professionalism. I had them done at a very nice graphic design store that does good work so they look great and that is half the battle in my opinion. Every little bit helps and you never know how you are going to end up attracting business sometimes.

Signage

I do have some signage out at my cabin and I'm sure that I've gotten a few drive-by clients who saw the sign, loved the area and who went online, found my cabin and inquired about booking it. It's a double edged sword to have signage on your property, on one hand it lets client's know they've arrived and it does let people know that the property is available for rent but it also let's burglars know that it's probably vacant from time to time. So you do need to be careful when putting out signage and you do need to be cognizant about the security of your property at all times.

I've also had neighbors who know that I rent my property have their summer guests inquire about my cabin instead of cramming a bunch of people into their homes with them. It works out nicely for everybody because they get to be near each other and visit with their family but don't have to sleep on couches or fold out beds and wake up every morning to a complete disaster. As they say, "Happy to see them come and even happier to see them go!" I always throw my neighbors a discount as an homage to my neighbors and it's appreciated.

Friends and Family

Sometimes when things are really slow (like for me, in April) or when you know that you aren't going to book a weekend you can advertise your place on Facebook. Facebook is probably the least desirable place to try to rent your property but sometimes you just never know. Most people who are really engaged in Facebook can have anywhere from 200 to 1000 friends and people do read their newsfeeds. There is always the chance that you might be able to rent out your place to one of your friends at a discount.

However, beyond that I've been known to offer the place up for free to a deserving friend or family member and just have them pay for the cleaning fee. This way there isn't anything out of my pocket, your family loves you for it and your cleaner gets another clean to help them stay busy through the slow months. This certainly isn't a money maker but it has to be at the very least beneficial from a karma standpoint.

<u>Craig's List</u>

Craig's List can be a good place to find some renters from time to time. When the vrbo just isn't coming through and it will happen from time to time you can always give Craig's List a shot. I have actually gotten renters that way and with Craig's List being free you really have nothing to lose by posting your place there. Additionally, if you have an account with Craig's List (which you should) you can place an ad with them and simply log into your account to renew it over and over again. Sometimes I've found that I've had to repost the photos but beyond that it's a very simple proposition and even though it might only net me a client or two a year that extra 1400 or so dollars that I can end up making from Craig's List pretty much pays for a nice little vacation or new appliances for the property or a portion thereof of some future remodel. It all adds up!

If you do all of these things there is little chance of not being successful as long as your property is competitively priced with like properties in the area.

<u>In conclusion</u>

VRBO is the single best thing I've found to draw clients to my cabin. There are other sites as well like Home Away Connect and Trip Advisor and so forth, but for me if something is working why would I need to have all those other sites? They are, perhaps, redundant.

Your VRBO site should also be considered a work in progress at all times. You should constantly be updating your photos if you have better ones, making sure your pricing is concurrent with the time of the year. Have photos for the different seasons of the year, don't hype your property with a snow scene heading into summer and vice versa. People see your snowy cabin picture in October and start getting excited for the winter holidays and skiing and now know what they are most likely going to see when they arrive during that particular season. Same thing goes for heading into the summer months, the sight of a beautiful property surrounded by trees covered in green leaves and the sight of expanses of green rolling hills or whatever your property provides - being viewed in the chilly spring months will also create some longing for your particular property and like they said in the movie 'Glengarry Glen Ross', "Always be closing", whether that is in writing or verbally or visually. Having great photos at all times is all part of the closing process, in fact sometimes you will close the client on your property before you even have to say a word!

6

Pricing and Price Points

Models and Calculations vs. trial and error

When I first went online with the very first property manager they came to the conclusion that I should charge $180 dollars per night which was them more or less understanding their market. Knowing this the actual "cost" to run my cabin per day at that time was around $90. Here is how I arrived at that figure.

Mortgage -	$2400 per month	80.00 Per night
Electricity -	$125 per month	4.15 Per night
Phone, Cable, Wi-Fi -	$95 per month	3.16 Per night

92.

Firewood @180 a cord (lasts 5 months)   1.20 Per night

Plowing, Landscaping, Hot tub maintenance –

700.00 per yr. on avg.   2.00 Per night

My cabin's first price-point

How my first property manager in Leavenworth first arrived at the $180 price point was a snap judgment on their part and of course I trusted them because I felt that they should know the market. But it was a very general amount that they were choosing to charge and it didn't at all take into consideration the time of the year, whether it was a weekend or a weekday, how many days the clients were going to stay and so on and so forth. What it also didn't take into consideration was whether or not I wished to be profitable or if I could rent the cabin out every single night of the month. The answers to those questions respectively were absolutely and not likely.   But then again, remember, they didn't really care whether I was profitable or not. They had an inventory of dozens of properties and either folks looking for a particular date would like my cabin at the current price or they wouldn't and if they didn't they would find another property in their system and they would then simply book a different one.

It didn't matter to them if my price point was always where it needed to be, they were going to make their money one way or another. They also refused to negotiate with a client on price, something I do all the time and it's important to note that sometimes it can be as little as reducing your price by $10 a night that makes the difference between getting a 600 dollar (2 or 3 day) booking or not.

Furthermore, to let you know, I don't just lay down for guests and let them pay whatever they want, I do have in my head what is acceptable to me and what isn't. More often than not I can arrive at a price with a client that ends up working for both parties and when it comes right down to it it's better to bring in "x" dollars minus 10% or 15% than to bring in nothing. At the end of the day I'm selling air. I'm not selling a manufactured good per se with a limited supply; the only thing that is actually limited is the number of days in the year and the more of those that you can book the better off that you will be in most cases.

What is also important to know is what your odds are to rent a particular weekend or weekday period. An example of this is that October and December weekends are always booked out to the nth degree. Therefore I have no reason whatsoever to discount and I pretty much refuse to because I know it's going to be booked. I will however reduce pricing just a bit for *guest performance*. For example, let's say that I'm going to charge $299 a night for the Oktoberfest weekend, a slight premium to my normal rates because it's a highly desirable weekend of the year. For a three night stay the price is going to be around 1000 dollars plus tax, more if they have a lot of guests coming with them as is often the case for those weekends (I charge $10 per guest for all guests beyond the first 2 as extra guests mean more laundry, more cleaning and more supplies used; it also means more people can chip up and at the same time stay together in the same place, something hotels cannot really offer).

What I will always do is knock off 5% if they can get their act together and lock down, book and pay for the rental within the next 24 hours or I'll simply lower the total price down to the next nearest large number i.e. I will lower a 799 dollar rate down to 750 even or thereabouts if they can book and pay before midnight that night or noon the next day. This typically spurs a client to action.

I've found if you don't do this they might hem and haw, keep looking on the VRBO for another place or just simply flake out and fall off of the face of the earth. But by discounting the price a bit, *in essence paying them to perform*, I find that I often get the booking and they get to lock down a place and everybody walks away a winner. Everybody loves a deal!

Figuring out your rack rate

In addition I think it's really important to figure out what your "rack rate" is going to be, a rack rate is basically the most that you can ever charge for a room or property and get away with it. Most hotel chains for example have a very high rack rate. An example of this used to be a sign that used to be on the back of hotel room doors. The sign would list, basically, the maximum price that one would have to pay for the room But by having a fairly high rack rate it would seem that these hotels could create the illusion that your special rate is actually quite reasonable by comparison.

Now I'm not suggesting that you create some ridiculously high rack rate and then try to charge folks a rate lower than that in an effort to dupe the client.

I think the best way to determine your rack rate is to consider what people would actually be willing to pay to stay at your property on the most desirable day of the year (for San Diego that might be the 4th of July, for Copper Mountain Colorado that might be New Year's Eve, so it depends on location). These are both times that everybody wants to be somewhere with their friends, nobody wants to drive, people like to be in the thick of the action and they will pay top dollar to split a hotel with their friends, have a great time, stay up all night and avoid a costly DUI charge. That therefore should be your rack rate.

95.

That said I also have my normal rates and these are very much rates that some people do not so much as blink when I tell them what that rate is going to be. But throughout the year I will run any number of specials and beyond those specials I will, again, throw people additional discounts to secure the deal.

When you have been selling as long as I have you know right away just by hearing the tone of a prospective guests voice whether they can pay the price, cannot pay the price, wish they could pay the price or simply wish the price was just a small amount lower. For the folks that do not stand a chance of paying it's typically best to bid them farewell and even go so far as to suggest some places in town that might be able to accommodate them, but really it's the prospective guests that you can tell simply wish the price was a bit lower, those are the people that you can negotiate with a little bit to create a win/win.

A good analogy for this is the car business. You can go and work at a Ferrari dealership where you might only sell 10 cars a year, but with the commissions being relatively strong in that market you might be able to make 6 figures selling 10 cars a year. On the other hand you could go and work at a Toyota dealership where you might sell that many cars a week. Sure your commissions are dramatically lower per car but at the end of the year you might even end up making more than the Ferrari salesman. Yes it's a lot more effort and paperwork and handholding and negotiating but the end result is pretty much the same. Another corollary is driving a cab. You can sit around waiting for the fare who needs a ride from downtown to the airport or you can drive around downtown taking folks a few blocks at a time and ringing the register all day long. The guy that makes the money is the guy who keeps his cab full with paying passengers throughout the course of his day, not the guy sitting at the airport in a long line of cabs waiting for that one passenger who needs to drive some crazy distance.

What's really terrible is when somebody waits at the airport all afternoon only to get someone who needs to go just a few miles, but enough with the analogies. My point here is that you keep your place rented; you charge an acceptable, profitable rate when you have to and you keep your cash flow flowing.

Normal pricing

Regarding normal pricing the secret is to find a price that makes sense to the bulk of your target demographic. What I've found for my cabin is that $249 a night on the weekends is about right and 199 on the weekdays also seems to work for most. How you arrive at your price will be a matter of guessing a bit in the beginning and then doing some fine tuning as time goes by. I find it interesting that I'm charging .5 percent of the appraised value of my property if I were to sell it turnkey. Whether or not that is a good gauge is hard to say, but it would mean that a million dollar home would go for about $500 per night which does sound about right.

Offering a free night

I also most times offer to give the third night free unless it's a holiday weekend. This is a real win/win for the guest and myself because typically I'm not going to rent out Thursday night or Sunday night anyway, the cabin would simply end up being empty and an empty cabin derives no revenue. But by offering to give a third night free it reduces the total cost of the clients stay because they are getting a free night, I'm getting the weekend guarantee ably booked and basically, I'm charging the guests full price. The guest feels they are getting a good deal on their three day stay (which they are) and everybody is happy.

97.

People who do stay during the week typically are quite flexible in their travel arrangements and just end up booking around my weekend guest's check ins and check outs. Things just typically seem to work out. There have been quite a few times when people want to stay for a period that intercedes with a period of time that I already have booked but that is the way it's going to go sometimes and really, at the end of the year, it all comes out in the wash.

Adjusting rates for the time of the year

During the slow months of April and May, I will reduce prices even further so that I can generate all the revenue that I can. There are always people that are looking for a getaway from the rainy, cold and dreary spring weather that we have in Seattle and even though it's not an ideal time to be in Leavenworth it's still better than the weather they are getting over in the city most days. So during the slow times I'll do 199 on the weekend and 125-150 a night during the week.

As far as your pricing goes you will find that, over time, you will fine tune it to perfection so that you are always deriving revenue, always staying booked and always at the very least getting your mortgage paid. I'm lucky in that I really only have two really slow months which again are sometimes late March, April and early May. I simply do the best that I can during those times. Also, if I've had any problems during the year with guests, like double bookings, or any other type of major problem, I will offer them a free night or even a weekend during those slow times of the year. (I've even gone so far as to create gift certificates with my properties logo in case of this very kind of event)

98.

Example of the Gift Certificate I've created......

THE CABIN AT EAGLE CREEK

Gift Certificate for the Cabin at Eagle Creek

*Pay to the Order of*_____

*In the Amount of*_____

*Valid Thru*_____

*Signed*_____

Since the property is going to be empty anyway, giving somebody a free stay during this time of the year really isn't going to cost you anything but maybe the cost to do the clean after the guests check out but can go a long way towards creating good will towards yourself and your property.)   Even though I'm not generating revenue in those cases I'm creating client loyalty. I also get a lot of maintenance done during those times of the year, I use those slow months to get the cabin all spruced up or conduct any larger construction projects that I've been looking to get done. Just like in our personal lives, when you have some downtime, use it productively to gear up for when things are once again busy.

During these slow times of the year I will also do trades with folks who provide a service that I want but that I really do not want to have to pay for. So I will offer a free weekend to my assistant at work, I'll offer my carpet cleaner to go and stay for the weekend in exchange for a free carpet clean (which is usually a $500 bill for me due to the amount of carpeting that I have in my house), my dog sitter, my CPA, my friends and family. The list goes on but considering a penny saved is a penny earned, working out deals during these times of the year is the same as deriving revenue. With that in mind I always make sure that these guests pay the cost of the cleaning which is usually 139 dollars. A small price to pay for them for a weekend out of town and it keeps me from having to pay anything out of my own pocket for their particular stay.

A last thought on pricing your property effectively. Try to identify 3 like properties in your area. Properties that are the same size, have the same amenities and are about the same distance to the nearest town. Then see what their pricing looks like and then check their calendars to see how busy they are and how many bookings they have. Pricing your property by the night is no different from pricing your property for sale, you really need to look at the comps (comparables) in the area. If you price to high you won't find a buyer, if you price to low you will sell your property in the first week and then kick yourself for not having started out asking for more. The secret is to price your property right so that you can garner business, compete with the properties in the area and above all be profitable.

In conclusion, find your perfect price point through trial and error, discount that around 20% for the weekdays. Run specials and discounts for the slow times of the year or consider trades. Offer a free night if you can agree with the client for them to pay full price for the weekend. Most guests can typically find a way to get a day off from work for a long weekend and lastly, keep your VRBO site updated at all times with current prices. The more that you are on VRBO perfecting pricing the more often prospective guests are going to be on your VRBO site taking advantage of the opportunity to stay at your place at a price that makes sense for them.

100.

7

The sales element

Now that you are running your own vacation rental, in essence your own business, you now have a product to sell, you have inventory (days) that you need to move and in the current competitive marketplace you are going to need to work on your selling ability and your negotiation skills.

<u>Anybody can become good in sales with a little practice</u>

I have been a fully commissioned salesperson since 2000 when I became a financial advisor for Morgan Stanley Dean Witter.

As my career progressed I moved on to work for WaMu Investments Inc. which later became Chase Investment Services Corp and then I want on to work in their niche market JP Morgan Private Client.

Prior to becoming a financial advisor I had made at least several attempts at sales and had failed each time. I think the problem with my previous attempts at sales was that during those previous stints becoming successful wasn't a matter of life or death. When I left my career with a major airline in 2000 to become a financial advisor it was a do or die proposition. Failure was not an option, nor was going back to the Airline and even though I had been told on a number of occasions that I would probably be very successful in sales if I ever gave it a try, somehow, I just didn't believe it.

Having come from a long line of Union Workers and hourly wage earners, most recently of course being my father who was an elevator construction worker, I just felt that I was predestined to be an hourly wage worker for the rest of my life because that was what my environment and genetics had been up to that point. What I would later find out, however, was that I was actually quite a good salesperson. And to me, after being in sales for such a long time, success in sales really boils down to a couple of things:

First, you much fully understand your product. As a financial advisor the product that I bring to the table is mostly myself. I'm selling my knowledge, years of experience, investment prowess, instincts and the products that I have at my disposal which are multitudinous. A client can make money in an up or down market depending on how you have your clients invested. Quite a few investments do well when the market isn't doing well, for example, bonds or perhaps the VIX index (volatility index). The nice thing about when I'm doing a sale for the rental of my cabin I'm selling something a bit more tangible. Also a major difference is in renting my cabin there is a limited supply of product. If a weekend is booked then that weekend is gone.

102.

With financial products, typically, there is an unlimited amount of that product that you can sell. The only thing in short supply is you, the amount of hours that you can work in a given day, week or month.

Additionally, anybody can sell X mutual fund to X client. I'm, however, the only one that can sell days at my cabin. So all things being equal going about sales for my cabin is much easier than what I actually have to do at work.

Also investments are usually sold and not purchased (except for perhaps some no load index funds and even those are typically, subconsciously, sold by Suzy Ormon) whereas the cabin oftentimes sells itself and when I say it sells itself what I mean is all the equity and sweat equity and personality that went into the cabin to make it be able to sell itself. When that does happen it's really nice and all I simply have to do is book the reservation for the guests. Other times it's not that easy and that's where having a little bit of a leg up in sales can be helpful.

This brings me to a point as well about positioning. Positioning your property can be quite important. I will mention this again throughout the book but basically you need to position yourself as somebody who is making their amazing vacation property or second home available to a few select individuals - not the masses. Sometimes the less desperate that I know I'm sounding the more likely I am to get the booking. There is something known as "cat string theory". Cat string theory is the understanding that when a string is just lying there on the floor the cat doesn't want to play with it but if you are teasing the cat with the string the cat goes wild trying to attack the string. Now I'm not saying to tease guests but there is nothing wrong with being discerning and not jumping all over the first person who wishes to rent your cabin over the Christmas holiday. The fact remains that if you are in the right area there will be more folks wanting that date than you will be able to shake a stick at especially as you get closer and closer to the date in question.

So in conclusion be engaging and engaged but relax and play back a little bit when you are having trouble locking a guest down and you might find them suddenly clamoring for your property. This might be especially effective when they are trying to negotiate you down while saying that they are looking at your property but also one other to see "who will give them the best deal". At this point I would never fail to mention that they aren't the only party considering renting my cabin for that particular period or at least days that are overlapping the days that they are trying to rent. There have been times that I've literally told some of these people to just go ahead and take the other place and within an hour they are back saying, "No, we'd rather take yours at your asking price, where do we pay?"

So here now are the most important things that I can tell you what I've learned about sales specifically as it pertains to running my cabin.

Understand and believe in your product

Don't just understand your product but also believe in your product! If you don't believe in your product or your price point for that product then you aren't going to do very well at all. People somehow know when you don't believe in and aren't passionate about your product.

Every product has a price point. Every property is going to have an appropriate price point whether it's a very basic one room ski shack or a multi-million dollar mansion. Those prices are going to differ greatly but if you have your price point correct then you will find buyers for your product. But you have to believe in your product and the only way to believe in your product is to bring the very best product that you can to the table. If you knowingly went cheap or perhaps "minimalistic" on your product then you aren't going to be confident in selling it.

Slumlords after all sell to the desperate and the income they receive is paltry compared to what they could receive if they were trying to sell a legitimate product.

On the other hand if you are knowingly renting out a ski shack and your price is right then you knowingly enter an agreement to accept very low payments from a client base that can afford your price and if it turns out you are happy and the client is happy then by and large that's a win/win.

Provide great customer service

Keep customer service as your focus and be a *consultative* seller. Help clients to understand why your place is going to be great for them. Talk up your properties attributes and downplay the negatives but always be honest. Be pleasant on the phone or in email with people. Help them with anything that they need help with and if you don't have the answer try to find it and get back to them.

For example, I had a group of girls coming in for a bachelorette party and they needed information on a good limo service to all the wineries in the area, something that I knew nothing about. In less than five minutes I Googled what I needed to Google and found a limo service that provided exactly the service that they were looking for. I could have simply told them to go and find this information for themselves but instead I did it for them, got them the name and phone number and came across both as knowledgeable, professional and caring. I would also venture to guess that, for the client, it sealed the deal and allowed me to book that weekend over some other opportunity. It's amazing the things that can be accomplished in a short period of time for your guests.

That said, if you are the type of person that is annoyed by answering questions then you are going to be at a disadvantage in this business. I've closed week long stays where I've brought in 2 grand by answering zero questions and/or going merely a few emails deep to get the guests on board. I've also gone 25 emails deep talking to a client about a two day stay.

It all comes out in the wash and more importantly the only thing that matters is what your net income is at the end of the year. If the emails do start to get a bit lengthy a quick way to deal with that is to simply say, "I'm ready to answer ALL of your questions at your leisure, please put them ALL into one email or better yet, just call me and I will answer them all at once, I'm super busy today at my other job but happy to help." Clients will get the point, finish up with their queries and move on. I've done this successfully but more importantly it doesn't happen often.

Responding to Inquiries

Promptly respond to Inquiries! Remember that most clients find a place or two or three that they are interested in. You will find this when you respond to clients by phone and they say, "Which property are you again?" So oftentimes you are going to need to respond to an inquiry within a half hour or so. If you are busy or tied up or what have just do all you can to respond to them as quickly as possible. I also try to call people first when they submit an inquiry if they've given me their phone number. Not all people do. If all you have is email then you are going to have to correspond that way. But you can explain a lot over the phone and also get a feeling for how much they are willing to spend. But if you are short for time you can always respond with a quick, "I got your request, I will be back with you in one hour, or whatever."

It lets them know you are aware of them. I will state this here and then again later but you really need to have a smart phone if you are going to have a competitive edge over your property peers. Smartphones most importantly have regular phone communications but also text and email. Being able to react to your inquiries in the moment as they come in is a huge advantage over those who do not. I also can respond to inquiries at 11 at night giving me an advantage even over some hotels or property management companies. It's nothing for me to respond to an inquiry or request at any point during my waking hours.

Communicating via email

As I mentioned, the most important thing that you can do is hit people back right away. The thing to remember is that people are going to look at your pictures and not read any of the verbiage that you've written about our property. So they are going to ask questions that will make you scratch your head like, "How much is it going to cost, or does your place have a roof on it or do we have to bring our own couch?"

To keep it simple and sweet and to get me on their radar I will create a new email, plug in their email address, type "cabin at eagle creek" in the tagline (there is an important reason for this). And then just simply say, "It's available, let me know how I can help you to book my cabin."

If the client says, "We want to book your cabin for these nights." I will respond with an email that leads them to my website's contact page (which you can see here shortly, or by going to www.cabinateaglecreek.com/contact) , on this page I have everything right there that the client could ever need in order to book their stay pretty much end to end. I have a PDF document that the clients can click on and open up (or even download) that has all of my payment instructions,

107.

my arrival letter or instruction manual for my cabin and my contract. Also on that page my prospective guests can also pay for their stay with my PayPal buy now button. I've made it a very seamless process.

The Rule of 3

If a client doesn't respond back to you in a timely fashion, keep track of them. About a day later after sending them an email with pricing and instructions get back to them with a simple email that says, "thoughts?" I would venture to say that you can do this about one or so more times and at that point if you still haven't heard from them then it's probably just time to let it go. Sometimes people do find another property and not every prospect is going to take the time to tell you they've gone in another direction. And that's OK; there are other fish in the sea.

When I send that email I've usually given the client their price and a deal of sorts to spur them to move forward quickly. So I'm hitting them back simply to say, "What are your thoughts here?"

Some folks appreciate the reminder and move forward, some say they found something else but are going to keep you in mind for the future, some don't reply but at least it again puts you back on their radar. The thing to remember is that everybody is different and is going to move forward in their own time.

Communication via telephone

On many occasion it's going to simply make sense to pick up the phone and call the client. If your VRBO inquiry is around a paragraph long or longer it's probably best to dial the client up. Otherwise you are going to end up shooting back and forth emails for weeks before you ever come to an agreement on anything.

Talking on the phone allows you to hash out all of the nitty- gritty details.

At the end of the conversation ensure that you ask. "Are you sure you don't have any other questions?" It's also good to refer them to your contract, arrival letter, payment instructions and VRBO information in full as all of those documents should contain just about everything that any client would ever want to know about location, pricing, distance to points of interest, directions, etc. There are those guests that do not enjoy the fine print or reading in general and therefore would rather simply hear it from you personally... and that's fine. Getting the booking is obviously critical and you are going to know in time who is a serious potential renter and who isn't.

<u>Be a concierge</u>

While speaking to guests, obviously be pleasant, courteous and informative. Help them with everything you can help them with as I've mentioned earlier. If you've ever chatted with a concierge in a hotel the thing you know about them is that they can arrange just about anything; reservations, spa services, transportation, sporting events and so forth. Take it upon yourself to be that person.

For example, I'm very good at finding things online, well, actually, Google is very good at finding things online, I'm good at Googling those things. If somebody wants to know about the distance to something or wishes to know of four good wineries in the area, I can find that data in 3 minutes or less call the client or prospect back with the info and almost guarantee-ably earn the booking by having done that. It's sometimes the little things that count.

As I say in my present career oftentimes, it's the point where you are asked a question by the prospect that you do not know the answer to when the meeting might come to an early conclusion. People want results and they want them from knowledgeable individuals. I'm lucky that even though I don't live in the area where my cabin sits that I know a lot about the area just from having explored so much of it. When I don't have the answer I find it immediately and provide a response. Sometimes it's simply the attentiveness to their needs that can make the difference.

A brief sidebar on Guest Comments

I'm going to sneak this in here because good guest comments are one of the greatest things that you can cultivate but can also turn into the bane of your existence if you aren't careful.

The thing to remember is that most guests are going to be great, especially if you have a nice place that you rent out at an "elevated" price. People who have a little bit of money to spend are usually going to treat your place with dignity and respect. When they check out they usually will take the time to email you back to say that they had a great time and when they do ask them to leave you a review on your VRBO website.   Most oftentimes they will leave a nice guest comment, especially if you make it easy enough for them to do so. The best way to do this is to send them an email asking them to do this with the link to the VRBO review section. Let them know how much it helps you to get more rentals in the future. You really need to be sure that they are going to give you a high rating before asking them. If there were troubles with your rental (code problems, key problems, lockout problems, equipment problems) it's probably best not to ask. Hopefully you've done everything you can to turn that situation around but you really do not want clients leaving mixed feedback about your rental.

As I've always said, "Praise publicly, criticize privately." Let the client vent through phone or email if there was an issue and then fix that issue. Do not let the situation evolve to where they are leaving you negative feedback on your VRBO site. Those comments are forever and can be very damaging.

With that in mind, be very careful when charging a client for damage and rule violations. You really have to consider just how much it is worth it in the long run. If the client knows they've done something wrong, admits they've done something wrong or if you have proof beyond a shadow of a doubt that they've done something wrong then you should charge them for their mistake but only if it cost you money or revenue and even then take into strong consideration what you are going after the client for. Remember that it's simply just good policy to not nickel and dime a client. Do not go after security deposits for the $4 broken glass or the $11 broken clock radio. Remember that sometimes things just break or fail. If you have a strong sense of what is fair you should be fine but you also simply need to remember that there is a cost of doing business.

Below is my current array of guest comments. Please go to www.vrbo.com/192335 for a better and full viewing of these pages.

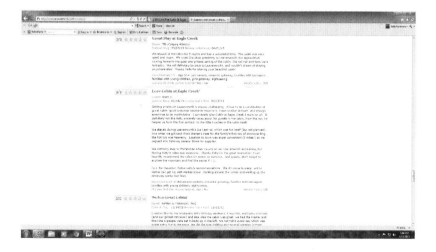

Be engaging

Although it's very important to be professional I think it's also important to be human and to have a sense of humor and to be engaging on the phone. It's also important to be brief and to the point and to be able to quickly add numbers in your head so that you can be driving down the road talking on your cell (with your wireless headset of course) and provide the clients with an out the door price for a certain period of days.

Also, out of the gate, try to create some kind of common ground with your client. If they are from Idaho and you've driven through their town on vacation, mention that. If they are a retired engineer for Boeing and you have an uncle who was a mechanic at Boeing, mention that. There is always common ground that you can find and when you can relate to your clients not only does it humanize you but it also instills the confidence necessary to allow the client to wish to move forward with you.

One very important thing to remember in this business is that you are either one of two kinds of people. And it's really how you establish your rental and how you navigate your way through the sales process. You are either a voice on the phone renting a unit aka a salesman selling a "cog" or you are *the owner of a second home who is offering the chance to share your property with a guest who is willing to pay you for the luxury of doing so (mentioned earlier in "positioning" but worth saying again in a different way.)* From my experience I've learned that the latter person in this scenario is going to blow away the former person in this scenario. And you can be either/or it just depends on how profitable you want to be.

Website

Beyond a shadow of a doubt I absolutely believe that a website is an absolute necessity.

112.

A website can draw traffic, sure, but beyond that it can be a completely functional place where prospective guests can view your property, check your calendar, consider your pricing, get directions and so forth. You can guide clients to your VRBO site and verse visa but you can also create a page, as I've mentioned, where your clients can book and pay, download documents for their stay and so forth. A website, beyond VRBO, is one of the greatest tools that you can have. One important thing is to ensure that your VRBO is linked to your website and that also your website is linked back to your VRBO website.

Putting together a website is fairly simple. I did not create my own but I did hire an excellent web designer to create mine for me and believe me when I say it was the best $700 I ever spent.

I looked at a bunch of other websites that she had created and basically stole the best ideas from other things that she had created. You are going to want something that looks modern, has nice, contemporary coloration and font and is organized in such a way that clients can navigate it easily.

When I was remodeling my cabin and painting each room I ended up painting the master bedroom a Ralph Lauren suede, moss green. Of all the rooms in my cabin that room, to me, seemed to have come out about the best. I liked that color so much that I ended up using it for my website, business cards and signage. The same might happen to you where you find a theme running through your property where you end up doing the same. Here are a few very important things that your website should contain. Remember that everything about this website from the colors and fonts, to the layout and the information are all going to be a huge reflection on your property, so spend the money and do it right!

1. Photos of your property that give the client a very clear picture of what they will be renting both inside and out

2. A map with directions on how to get to your property.

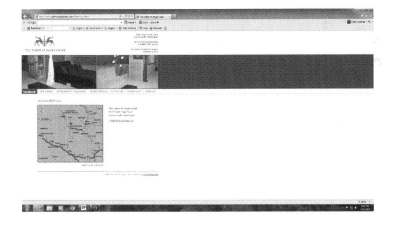

3. At least several ways for the client to get ahold of you, my suggestion, phone number, email, and fax number.

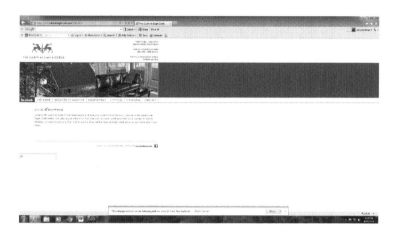

Links to VRBO, your calendar and your Facebook page. If a client wants to book right away then having these various links can help them to do that in a very easy and simple fashion. It also lets them know if the days they are looking for are available. A link to your properties Facebook page might also provide them with some additional photos and perhaps some additional comments from guests who've stayed there.

115.

4. One of the best inclusions that I've made in the last 5 years to my website was a "buy now" button which allows people to pay me via PayPal, either through their PayPal account or with a credit card. This is pretty easy to set up. First you have to establish a PayPal account. Doing this is easy enough and again another website that will walk you through their process.

5. Once this account is established you have to set up your "buy now button". That is not only going to be just a little bit more complicated but also it's going to most likely need to be applied to your website by your website designer. It's not a big deal and simply implies that they are going to need to add a file to your website.

116.

And again, when running your property on your own, any time that you can streamline something or remove yourself from an equation is always good. I have truly done a thousand dollar booking with one single email response verifying pricing but with zero additional communication or interactions and this is something that can be accomplished with the kind of streamlining I'm talking about.

Picture of my contact page with buy now button and welcome link below:

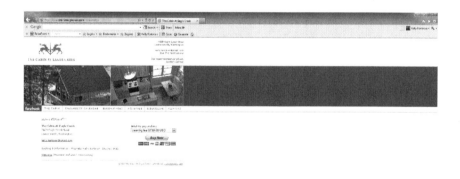

Arrival Letter

Here is my arrival letter in its entirety. The goal of the arrival letter is to provide the client's with a working guide of your property so that anything that they might ever need to know they can find in the arrival letter. The less that they have to call you the more free time you have to do other things.

I've tried to lay everything out in the arrival letter in a way that makes sense based on the number one things they will be doing once they arrive to the little things they are going to need to do upon departure and then everything in between.

It is a continual work in progress though because just when you think that you've addressed everything something new pops up that alerts you to the fact that you need to go back in and change some of the language again. This is where mine has arrived after 5 years of making adjustments to it.

Arrival letter from start to finish

THE CABIN AT EAGLE CREEK

Important websites
http://www.facebook.com/home.php#/pages/Leavenworth-WA/The-Cabin-at-Eagle-Creek/94586792957
check out our new Facebook page!
http://www.cabinateaglecreek.com/contact.htm
pay online using the link above via our PayPal button!

Thank you again for choosing to stay at The Cabin at Eagle Creek. We hope you will enjoy your stay, relax and find whatever adventure you seek. This is very important information and we ask that you read this in its entirety; it will provide you with a more peaceful and safe stay while at the cabin.

**Please print out this document and take it with you to the cabin as it instructs you on
how to function while you are there. Please fill out and sign contract (very easy to
do) and send along with a wet signature to the address provided on the contract,
thank you very much!**

You will find information on the following:

Directions, Door Codes and Alarm Codes, Dog rules, Driveway tips, Fireplace
Instructions, etc.

Many of the questions you may have can also be answered the
website www.cabinateaglecreek.com or you may call with further questions.

Directions:

It's very easy to find once you've arrived in Leavenworth on Hwy 2 (from Seattle-
heading East) you will make a left onto the Chumstick Hwy, go several miles until
you go under a train-trestle/bridge. Shortly thereafter you will see Eagle Creek Road
on your right hand side and signs to the Eagle Creek Winery and Eagle Creek Stables
where you will make a right. Travel several miles down that road until you pass the
Winery. The cabin is about the fifth or sixth driveway past the winery on the left
hand side. **9820 Eagle Creek Drive.**

Surveillance Cameras

We now have also added surveillance cameras to protect the cabin when it is
unoccupied. **Do not worry, the cameras only point at the front door and out the back
door.** The cameras connect to a DVR that records several weeks of data then re loops.
**It is merely in the event of a theft or break in that we would be looking at the
tape.** We do not transmit the camera data anywhere.

Please note that we want you to feel safe and happy and to have a great time out there
so please know that we are not monitoring your activities while you are out there.

**(Also, note, that if you were to shine a flashlight into the dome of the camera in the
living area you will clearly see that the camera points out the window towards the
deck where one might wish to try to break in)**

Television and Internet:

We have three televisions, a flat screen TV a big screen TV and a Sony flat screen
television, we offer DirecTV. If you would like to order movies please call DirecTV

and give them your credit card information. Please do not bill them to the cabin as there is a **$50 surcharge for doing so** as we have to go through the bill, see who stayed at the cabin at that time then track you down for the money since we will have already credited your security deposit.

Internet is now available and the **code to use the internet** is on the modem behind the wine rack in the kitchen.

Cell phone signal is sporadic depending on your carrier. If you wish have your phone calls forwarded to the house phone at **509 548 0294.**

Door Codes and Alarm Codes:

The front door code, along with the alarm code, will be provided to you just prior to your arrival. The front door is easy to operate just press the "Schlage" button on top then the code, the door will unlock. The door automatically locks in about two seconds, be sure to keep the code with you in case you get locked out or forget.

The cabin also has an alarm.

It is important that you arm the alarm upon leaving the cabin for any length of time and disarm it upon your return. It is, again, very easy to operate and takes five seconds to arm and disarm. Here are the instructions. The alarm company knows each time the alarm is armed and disarmed, if something goes missing during your stay as a result of the alarm not having been armed you are liable so please arm the alarm when leaving the cabin for daytrips or evenings out.

Upon opening the door you will have thirty seconds to get to the code box which is right by the door. (The door code and the alarm code will always be the same) You are going to hit the entry code (again provided with the code for the door) then the number 1. Upon departure you are going to hit the code again then the number 2, quickly without pause.

When arming the alarm for the day be sure to either take your pet with you or if leaving your pet behind you will want to put them either out on the deck or in their crate upstairs. Otherwise the motion detector may be set off.

We conduct a complete inventory of everything both prior to your stay and after your departure. Please see rental contract for more details regarding this. We simply ask that you partner with us in ensuring that all of our items, furnishings and possessions remain in the cabin upon your departure. Thank you! On the counter you will also find a guest log, please sign in and tell us how your stay went! It would also be great if you could log back onto www.vrbo.com/192335 and leave comments so other guests know how you enjoyed your stay.

Dog Rules:

If you are bringing a dog, here is a reminder of some common sense rules.
Try to keep your dog in the downstairs area only.

Also please keep your pets off of the furniture and the beds as the comforter covers are not dog hair or drool friendly.
Keep an eye on your dog when you let them out the door, there isn't a fence at the cabin and there is a road nearby that cars sometimes zip on down.
Let your dogs out often so they do not pee inside.
Weather permitting keep your dog out on the deck or in a crate when you are heading into town without them.
Some dogs are puppies longer than others, so please keep those who take longer to "grow-up" crated when you leave or when you cannot keep a constant eye on them.
We do not allow cats as we are both very allergic to them. Do not throw balls inside the house and try to feed them and give them treats outside or on the deck.

Pick up after your dog please. This is not in the cleaners list of things to do between guests. If the cleaner has to pick up after your stay and he will check after each stay we will charge you **$25** for doing so. This is the least favorite part of his job and he charges me accordingly! Sometimes during heavy snows and then melt offs, dog droppings may appear and it might be hard to discern what belonged to your dog, just please do all you can to help us here. It's greatly appreciated and the next guest appreciates it also.

Driveway Instructions: (wintertime only)

Leavenworth is a snowy and wintry wonderland. My driveway is no exception. The driveway is tackled with a plow before every stay and occasionally during your stay if there is significant snow. It is a bit steep and like every other driveway and road in Leavenworth you cannot get down to the pavement with plowing alone. Therefore try to bring your SUV or rent an SUV or other four-wheel drive vehicle before coming out in the wintertime. To get up the hill be in four wheel drive in a low setting. Get a bit of a head start and maneuver up the hill, momentum is your friend; park in the top level area. Turn around to head down and be sure to tap your break if you do not have anti lock brakes.

If you are not comfortable doing this, or not solid behind the wheel of a four wheel drive vehicle then **park at the bottom of the driveway.** Yes it's a 30 yard walk to the door but our goal is your safety.

Fireplace Instructions:

Start your fire with a fire-starter and some kindling. **Keep the doors of the fireplace closed until the fire is very hot and the smoke has cleared otherwise the cabin will fill with smoke.** Keep the wood towards the back of the fireplace. Do not burn paper, magazines or other garbage in the fireplace. This creates a ton of smoke.

TWO fire-starters are provided for your use at the beginning of your stay and more can be purchased in town. When the fire is going nicely open the doors but make sure you put the screen back up in front of the fireplace. If the cabin is still smoky close doors once more until it appears that the smoke has again cleared.

We have just replaced the fireplace glass at $225 per pane with a ceramic resin glass. It's pretty sturdy but will not withstand large fiery logs falling on it and staying there. Therefore it is imperative that you:
Monitor your fire
Keep the logs to the back of the fireplace (which helps with smoke also)
Do not stack wood too high
Do not go to bed with a large fire going
Any time the glass has broken in the past it's been due to large logs falling on the glass while ignited. **This is easily preventable. If the glass is broken during your stay we will charge your security deposit for replacement.**

Hot Tub Instructions:

The hot tub runs perpetually. I know that 98% of you know this but for those who do not, please do not feel the need to turn the hot tub off or on at the wall breaker. It could damage the tub. If you have any problems at all with the hot tub while you are staying there please contact **my assistant Lisa Foster on his cell phone.**

If you turn off the spa at the breaker and it causes any damage whatsoever your security deposit will be charged for repairs. The breaker for the spa is marked "only touch in case of emergency" please take our request to not touch the breaker seriously.

Typical damage from a tampered breaker are frozen pipes, frozen pumps, frozen heaters, inability to restart spa, damaged to sensors, damage to electrical systems and the list goes on and on. 95% of all spa troubles begin and end with guests tampering with the breaker. Please do not touch unless of an emergency.

Also please be careful when adjusting the spa and it's temperature. There is a mode button on the spa that offers a sleep mode. Do not put it in this mode as the spa will stop heating. If you see 5L on the Spa please hit mode until it says 5t. This keeps spa at 104 or desired temp at all times.

Do not leave children unattended in spa for even one second. All persons under 16 must be accompanied at all times. The other 5% of the time when spa damage has occurred it's been when small children have been in the tub unattended. Please help here as well.

Finally the hot tub is a great accessory for the cabin and we are glad to provide it we just ask that you help us in keeping it clean and functional.

Not having read the rules is not an excuse for a spa mishap.

Take a shower if you are dirty, sweaty, etc. before entering the tub. We keep a small amount of clarifier above the washing machine if you would like to add some at the end of the night, the spa will be clean when you wake up in the morning.

Make sure that the hot tub cover is on the spa when not in use. If it is windy, consider grabbing a couple of clean round rocks to put on the cover or latch down with straps.

Turn Spa to 104 degrees after you check out if you've turned it down for any reason.

Before checking out ensure that the spa is still running and check the breaker on the wall that nobody has turned the spa off. It's important that the spa is kept running.

We keep extra spa chemicals above the washer and dryer. Make sure that bromine floater stays full. If bromine dissolves away and the spa is continually used you will get spa rash which is itchy and unpleasant but not life threatening. Who wants to be itchy and unpleasant in such a romantic location, right?

Before you go to bed at night:

Make sure the **fire in the fireplace is out.** For your comfort, you may want to turn the heat down to 60 and perhaps even open all the doors in the cabin for 5 minutes. Let some cool air in, even in the wintertime. The heat rises in the cabin so if it's 70 downstairs it's about 80 upstairs. With all the flannel sheets and down comforters you are going to be plenty warm! If you do not do this the folks upstairs are going to be quite toasty!

Checkout instructions:

Our cleaner spends about three hours cleaning between stays. Here is all we ask of you before checking out:

- **Put all dishes in the dishwasher** and run, dishwasher tablets are provided below the sink.
- Take the sheets off of the used beds and **place downstairs next to the washer.**
  We leave a lint brush in the cabinet beneath the coffee pot, use it to remove excessive dog hair, it could save you having to pay a fine!
- Turn the heat down to **60 degrees** in the wintertime and turn the air up to **75 degrees** in the summertime.
- Leave a light on somewhere in the house.
- Make sure the **hot-tub cover** is on securely and the hot-tub strap is secure.
- Bag up garbage and place in the garbage bin provided either outside the door or **down by the road**, garbage folks come early Monday morning around 6:30.
- Make sure, if you use the BBQ grill, that you **turn the propane off at the tank** each time as it leaks otherwise. Scrape down the grill as best as you can, it's appreciated. This is much easier to scrape when hot then when cold, more sanitary for next guest also.
- Make sure that your fire is out before heading home; avoid using water if at all possible.
- Sign the **guest-log** and let us know how your stay went.
- Make sure all doors and **windows are locked and bolted** and make sure the alarm is armed, put the key back in the key-box and tumble the code.

Please note in contract the levies and fines for noncompliance, we want you to get your full security deposit back!

Checkout Checklist Our Cleaners Use

Condition of cabin scale of 1-10 _____

Dishes in dishwasher   Y / N _____

Dog Hair on bedding   Y / N (if so excessive?) _____

Sheets lying near washer? Y / N _____

Inventory Done?   Y / N deficiencies? _____

Hot Tub condition scale of 1-10_____

Cigarette Butts / Smell   Y / N degree? _____

Grill brushed down?   Y/ N _____

Garbage down by road?   Y/ N_____

Notes/ Misc.:

_____

_____

_____

Friendly Reminders:

In the past, we've had some minor complaints from the neighbors of rowdiness and loudness with some renters. Our policy is in your signed contract, but as a reminder, we ask that you kindly cease all outdoor play by midnight; including hot tub use. Our neighbors do have our contact numbers as well as our property assistants (who drives past the cabin on her way home from work in Leavenworth each night) and should we be contacted by a neighbor, and a phone call or visit is to be made to the house, you will be charged $50 for time and you risk the chance of being evicted. Also, you may NOT at any given time, go over the allotted maximum number of guests per your signed contract, even for a "day visit". This can be cause for termination of your stay. All that said 99% of our renters have been truly awesome, this is for the 1% that have broken the rules, upset the neighbors and walked off with cabin items.

Lastly, should you be in need of anything, please contact me and I will happily assist you!

Thanks and enjoy your stay!

Warmest Regards,

Kelly Kortman

* Note, I will give a client all the time in the world that they need on the phone etc. but for some folks they really don't even want the human interaction, they just want to get it done, book it and call it a day. I'm convinced that adding this link was one of the best moves that I've ever made and one of the best ideas that I've ever thought up.

125.

As you can see a website can accomplish many things for you. It can help you to market and advertise your property, it can further help you to close sales, it can assist the guest with concierge type questions and also help you to get your clients booked and really whatever else you wish to make of it. In the internet age that we live in a free standing website is pretty much a must have.

Tools necessary to be an effective Vacation Rental Property Manager

Most of these things are patently obvious but these things still need to be said. (If you are online savvy then please skip ahead) If you are not effective with the below tools or at least willing to try to become effective at using these technologies then you should simply go out and hire a property manager, but to be on the VRBO you, as mentioned earlier, you really need to have the following:

Computer – If you are going to run your vacation rental on your own you are going to need a computer. Being able to access the VRBO site is obviously critical. It's where you are going to be generating your referrals, updating your calendar, responding to inquiries and so forth. My VRBO inquiries not only show up on my VRBO site but they are also sent to my email. When I receive an email it goes to my "smartphone" which then pings me to let me know that an email has arrived into my inbox. Once I am alerted to the email I once again try to respond asap.

E-mail - Email is a great way to communicate with your guests and prospective guests. If you work full time as I do you are going to need a way to get in contact with people at your earliest convenience and email does just that.

Also all of your inquiries are going to be sent to you via email. Turning on your computer and functioning within the confines of email is about the easiest thing that you can do on a computer once you figure out the basics.

I also highly recommend using **Gmail** for all of your email needs. The reason for this several fold; number one Gmail has an excellent <u>spam filter</u> so that when your emails are going to your smart phone or I-phone all of the garbage emails are filtered out. As the years go by and spammers and marketers get your email you are going to be receiving a ton of spam and other forms of junk mail. You really want to be able to filter all of that out so that you can just focus on the emails that are coming in that are important. But most importantly, they have an excellent search field so that you can search and scan your emails for important key words. An example of this is that when I respond to VRBO inquiries I always open a new email and put "cabin at eagle creek" in the title of my email. This way later I can put those words into the search field and pull up all of the people that I've emailed about my cabin. This can help me to find those who have responded, who have not responded and so forth. It also allows me to run through that list and cross reference that with my calendar to ensure that I have everybody booked in and that I do not have any double bookings.

I can also just simply put in the word "VRBO" and it will pull up all of my vrbo inquiries. This is another way to ensure that I've contacted or re-contacted everybody.

So in conclusion if you don't have Gmail, sign up for it. I do believe that it's a great attribute for communicating with guests and staying organized. Having a "smartphone" to send all those emails to gives you a chance to respond to guests in a prompt fashion when you are away from home which in this day and age is, let's face it, most of the time.

My streamlined booking process, end to end

In conclusion here is how my booking process usually goes now from start to finish.

1. The prospective guest finds my property on the VRBO website. (Although sometimes they may find it through Craig's list or through word of mouth or perhaps they are a repeat). Once finding my property and identifying it as the place where they may like to stay they then send me an inquiry with their dates and usually a request for a price.
2. The inquiry immediately goes to my email inbox which then pushes that information to my cell phone where upon arrival I will usually be provided both a visual alert and a sound alert (my phone makes a dinging sound).
3. I look at the inquiry and ensure that those dates are available. Most times they are. I will then immediately provide them with a response that it's available and a quote. I do have a preformatted email that says the following:

Dear Guest,

Thanks for your inquiry; we'd love to have you! 99% of the time my calendar is up to date so if it's showing available you are most likely good to go. The rate for that time-frame is XXX. But if you book by midnight I will lower it to XXX just to create a win-win.

To book and pay go to cabinateaglecreek.com/contact here you will find my PayPal Buy Now button. You will also find my welcome link in the bottom left hand corner.

The welcome link will open a Word or PDF document that contains payment instructions, arrival letter (how to function while out at the cabin) and the contract. Once you've paid we will block those days out for you.

Once we have your filled out and signed contract (in it's entirety) and your $300 security deposit we will get you the codes to get in and get through the alarm.

Most everything is designed to go seamlessly, however, if you need my help you can call me on my cell at 206 992 1822 or at home at 360 297 3195.

Questions, let me know,

Kelly Kortman

Owner TCAEC

4. Once the client reads this response email they usually start thinking about whether they are truly ready to spring into action and book the cabin. Other times they may have to start getting their friends together and other times still they might have to deliberate on whether or not that is the price they are willing or can afford to pay. If they decide they wish to move forward then they can simply do that with the instructions I've provided. If they need me to walk them through they usually call me or email me back with additional questions.
5. If the guest is resourceful they usually just figure things out and then send me the payment. At this point the client will usually use the buy now button and pay.

129.

6. When this happens I receive an email from PayPal that shows up on my phone that I've received money and from whom and for how much. If I have time in the moment I will then log into PayPal and move those funds into my checking account electronically (or through the ACH system otherwise known as Automated Clearing House.)

7. Depending on how far the guests stay is into the future the client will mail me their signed contract (pulled out of the welcome link), scan it and email it to me or sometimes fax me the filled out and signed contract. If the guest and I are short for time then the guest will sometimes just PayPal me the security deposit as well which I will then refund to them upon a successful checkout. If there is plenty of time before there stay though I will just have them send me their security deposit check which I hold in my safe at home and then upon their successful check out I will then simply shred the check. Sometimes guests want verification that their check has been shredded at which point I will write VOID across their check, rip it in half, take a photo of it and then email them a picture of that camera phone photo. That process takes 15 seconds and is a lot easier and cleaner than sending a client back a copy of their voided check. Again, I'm all about streamlining things and trying to make it easier on everybody.

8. After the payment has been received on PayPal I immediately try to block the days out on my calendar and let the clients know I've done that. This makes them feel better and I know that I've got those days blocked out and now I'm not at risk of double booking those days.

9. Once I've received the contract and the security deposit, usually through the US Mail, I will call the client and give them the door and alarm code. If it turns out that I do not get around to doing this for some reason I've already let the client know at some point during our conversation that they may need to call me prior to their stay to get their alarm and door codes.

130.

10. This typically ends up being done through email. Upon receiving their request I will always check my calendar to make sure that everything is in good order, there is no double booking and that I have all their stuff. Therefore giving the guest the codes right before there stay is a good way to be reminded of who is coming and when. I will usually cc: my house cleaner with the email response to ensure we are on the same sheet of paper with the door and alarm code. If it turns out I'm wrong then she can address that right then and there.

11. At this point the guest now has everything and I now have everything. The guest then comes and stays and more often than not, everything goes great.

12. After the guest checks out my cleaner heads out to the property to conduct the clean. While she is doing that she is also performing an inventory of all of my household goods for damage or missing items. If all is in good order she gives me the thumbs up and I send the client back their security deposit or destroy their security deposit check. Sometimes a guest will follow up to ensure that that has been done and sometimes they do not.

13. After the stay I will most times follow up with the guest to get some feedback from them. Many times guests will fill out my guest log at the cabin. Sometimes they will not. I always like to know where I stand with my guests so a quick email follow up can be helpful to see how we are doing. If the guest says that everything is great I will usually send them the link to my comments section of my VRBO site. The more good comments that you have the better. If there was something that didn't go well for them I will fix it immediately and then follow up with them to let them know it's been fixed. This might be overboard but I don't care too much about being overboard in a good way. The link to the comments section is as follows:
http://www.vrbo.com/192335/reviews/write

131.

This entire process from start to finish usually takes about 5-15 minutes out of my life. Because everything is already created and out there for people to access the only thing I really ever have to do is negotiate, barter or follow up with clients regarding their stay.

I usually just send my cleaner the check in and check out dates for my guests once a month and of course I will email her if we get last minute bookings. She invoices me for her work and the purchase of any supplies and I pay her when I pay the rest of my bills.

In conclusion, just like with anything else, something is only hard until you've done it a bunch of times and then it becomes so automatic you don't even think about it anymore.

Take driving for example. The first time in your life that you drive a car down a busy road your hands are in a death grip on the steering wheel and you are white knuckling it the whole way down main street thinking you are going to sideswipe a car at any moment. Cut to a few years later and you are driving down the road, drinking a coffee, talking through your blue tooth, bottle feeding a baby in the back seat and changing the radio dial. There is really no difference between that scenario and this one right here. The truth remains, 6 years ago I didn't know a single thing about property management and now, lo and behold, I'm writing a book about it.

8

Negotiations With Prospective Guests

Learn How to Barter

One aspect of the sales process is to be able to successfully negotiate with people. If you've ever been in a foreign country and tried to barter for something then you know what this process entails to a small degree. When you post your prices on the VRBO site, people are going to be seeing the general gist of what you are trying to charge for your property for that particular week, month or even, time of the year.

However, almost everybody wants to try to negotiate a lower price. My secret is to beat them to the punch which I go on to describe below.

As the years go by you will learn which weekends are worth negotiating over and which ones you will eventually almost always rent out. Once you know which weeks or months or weekends are historically slow then you can begin to adjust your rates and be willing to negotiate accordingly. You will also learn in time what your absolute bottom line pricing is as well. For myself, as I've mentioned before, is usually about 125 dollars a night which doesn't include clean or tax. When people try to negotiate below that bottom line price it can make me quite skeptical. I begin to ask questions like, are they bartering me down because they are young and really cannot afford it and if so in what condition are they going to leave my place or is this party just insanely cheap, that also raises a number of questions like "will they begrudgingly pay the price but feel that that price must have also included all of my bathroom towels?"

In this business you are going to find yourself running into an interesting array of characters. Now don't get me wrong, 95% of all inquiries are going to be awesome and will simply pay the price for that time of year. But there are a few different types of people that you should become adept at handling so that you can still lock down the deal and here they are.

You are going to be dealing from time to time with the chronically cheap, those who want to stay at the super nice place but don't want to pay the price or just simply want to barter you into oblivion. Then there are those that just love the dance that is associated with the bartering process, although these people I sometimes feel would have way more fun visiting the tiny craft shops of Mexico than to spend all their time bartering with me on the phone. Simply put they love to talk you down from your posted prices just for the sake of talking you down from your posted prices.

Additionally you also have the young and broke (or sometimes rarely the middle age or elderly and broke) or the carefree, vagabond types who meander from town to town living out of a backpack in perpetuity.

There are a host of other types but the last type is the "hey buddy, we are going to leave it cleaner than when we got there." types which also coincides with the "hey man, we are going to advertise your place to all our awesome friends and we are going to come back again and again" types.

The secret in dealing with all of these people is to let them know your bottom line price for that weekend based on your history of renting that particular weekend out. Either they will get on board or they will fall to the wayside, one last thing. Never feel bad or let anyone make you feel bad for the price that you are charging for your property. I've had people tell me, basically, that I was a bad person for charging so much or not negotiating with them further or not honoring their price because of their predicament. That isn't your job. It's actually on them to find a place that is in their price range. I couldn't afford to stay at a Motel 5 when I was in my late teens (and by Motel 5 what I mean is it was a motel 6 until one of the rooms burned to the ground). I certainly didn't call some out of my price range property and tell them that it was their responsibility to rent me their place at a price that I was willing to pay.

Encouraging people to act

Here is how you deal with those who need to barter. Again everybody wants a deal and you want to get a booking and lock down some cash flow,

135.

And therefore I will offer them a 10%, or depending on the time of the year maybe even a 15% or 20% discount off of posted prices if they pay me before midnight that night (even 15% off of a 700 dollar deal (cost of a typical long weekend) is only going to cost me 105 dollar but flip that on it's head and I've just brought in 595 dollars that I might not have received otherwise, right?

Therefore what I get from them is performance, I get money right away if they can get their act together quickly enough and I lock down the guests, I know the weekend is booked and I can move onto bigger and better things. Now if they still want to hem and haw after that, more power to them, but what I will simply say to them is that at 12:01 I'm reverting back to my normal pricing because "based on history I've always been able to book that particular weekend out." (That statement of course, should be historically true.)

Which is another good point, charge a little bit more than you think you should in your advertised pricing, 10 or 20 dollars per night, if they fall in love with the pictures of your place and are secretly dying to stay there and then you throw them a 10% discount you will most times lock in the client. So my point here is to give yourself some wiggle room. This is no secret here; people have been doing it for as long as things have been being sold. And if you do discount ask for something in return, the best thing I've thought of is prompt payment. I also do not take partial payments or security deposits; if you want to book my property out you simply have to pay me in full.

I have taken partial payments from time to time and normally it's a rough road. You have to spend a lot of time chasing down the client for the final payment, sometimes they forget and God forbid you are the one who forgets and doesn't realize it until after the client has stayed because good luck getting your money then!

In conclusion this is one of the most valuable things that I've learned. Provide people with a discount but only if they take action immediately.

Posted rates and discounting

Obviously I have my rates posted on my VRBO site. My posted rates are higher than what I would most often deem an acceptable rate for a given time of the year.

When responding to clients via email or by phone I will lay out *what the price would be if* they were paying the full rate or the posted rate. But I will be quick to point out that if they can pay within the next 24 hours that I will reduce it a bit. Usually I will find the next lowest even number. So therefore if the price came in at 699 I might reduce that to 650, if the total price out the door came to 1478 I might consider lowering it to 1400 or even 1350. My posted "discounted" rates are of course much better than my rack rates as well. Then I point out how much money they would be saving by booking today.

If it turns out that they simply cannot act that quickly then I will throw them a slightly higher price if they can get it together in a week's time and then I will also simply tell them that if they cannot meet either of those parameters then I will still try to do something for them at the point that they can actually move forward with the booking but that it's not going be as good as either of those two prices and there is also a chance that by the time that we reach that date in the future the place could be long booked by then.

I do think that I am fairly priced and the thing that does give me some leverage, which will be discussed later in this book, is the fact that I have rave reviews on VRBO for my cabin. People will pay a little bit more for a place that has rave reviews.

137.

I've never received less than a 5 star rating, ever. It is also true that a few bad ratings, or worse, no ratings at all can hurt you.

I also advise purchasing a guest book like the one that I have at my cabin to get the reviews rolling as you can add them yourself from your guest log although, to a guest, they might carry slightly less weight than a guest comment left directly on your website from the guest themselves, nevertheless, they are still something.

If a client does come back weeks later it usually means that they really want your place and oftentimes they will ask if I will still honor that earlier discounted rate. If the weekend is still open and I don't have any nibbles from anybody else for that weekend I will offer them something that is pretty close to the earlier discounted rate but not exactly. After all, every time that a client comes back and takes some time from you then you should get some type of compensation for the time that you've given them.

138.

I would guess that 7 or 8 in 10 times you can get the client to move forward immediately. In 1 or 2 in 10 times they will still act but it might take just a little bit longer. And then 1 in 10 times the client won't come back at all or they will find another place. Larger parties are sometimes harder to lock down than smaller parties but not always. If there is one person in the lead role trying to get 8 other people's acts together then it can sometimes end up being a little bit more challenging.

Cleaning on the way out

   Another tactic that I will employ to help people to get to a lower price point is to have the client do the majority of the clean. From time to time you will have clients straight up say, "Oh, we promise, we will leave the cabin better than we found it." I simply say, "Ok, but if you don't then we are going to charge your security deposit for the things that weren't cleaned to our specifications, however, if you follow through, then sure, we can charge you half or so of the normal cleaning fee to give you a break." If they do follow through this can save the clients about another 50 bucks, therefore if people don't mind cleaning on their last day of vacation then that is fine with me. We do ask all guests to run the dishes through the dishwasher, to strip the beds and to run one load of wash, preferable towels so that we can begin drying those the minute we walk through the door to start our clean. Often-times too my cleaner will simply take sheets home so that she isn't just sitting around the house waiting for things to dry with nothing left to do. (This is why it's important to have two or three sets of sheets for each bed in the house).

   Obviously we want all of our clients to walk around the house and put every bit of garbage into the garbage can and then to bring that can down to the Waste Management can that we keep down at the street.

If they do these things then all we have to do is finish up the wash, wipe down and sanitize everything, sometimes clean up a little fireplace debris if they were having fires in the cabin, make the beds and lastly do the floors.

My cleaner also takes care of my hot tub so while things are coming together inside (sheets drying) I will have her check the spa water quality and add chemicals. I also have her do a walk around to pull any obnoxious weeds or dandelions, check for dog droppings (probably the worst part of her job but something that needs to be done) and hose off the outside deck when necessary.

Every couple of weeks I will have her pressure spray the driveway to get rid of loose bark, dirt, tire tracks or whatever else ends up on the asphalt. Long story short the goal is to get your cleaner in and out in under three hours, if the time necessary to clean the cabin goes beyond that that is usually when I might end up being charged extra by her. When these times occur it's important for your cleaner to document why she had to stay for such an extended period of time. If you have her on a special project that is one thing, (spring cleaning for example) but if it is simply due to guest negligence then it is important to know about that because at that point the added cost should fall on the client that just checked out and left your place in complete disarray.

Knowing when to cease bartering and wishing a prospect well

If the guest cannot agree with the price offered, pay right away or aren't interested in cleaning and continue to wish to barter below your "break-even" price point then sometimes you just have to do the following:

Put things in perspective by saying something to the effect of, "You know, I think what you are looking for really at that price range is the (fill in blank based on what price they are asking for) Best Western, Holiday Inn, Rodeway Inn or Motel 6 in town."

My feeling is this, if you want to pay $90 a night in Leavenworth, Washington or $60 dollars a night in Punxsutawney, Pennsylvania then you are going to either get a vacation rental that is old and antiquated with worn furnishings and a black and white TV with an antenna, or you are going to get two beds in one room with a TV and a nightstand. My second point to this is that the moment that you recommend that they stay at another location they know that the negotiations are over which of course immediately tilts everything back in your favor. There has to be a price point that you have no desire to negotiate below understanding that this is going to vary based on the time of the year. Otherwise people hearing the hesitancy in your voice will continue to try to barter. Then inevitably, in your quest for any kind of revenue you will miss out on a client willing to pay full price.

For those that simply love to dicker (sometimes you can just hear it in their voice from the moment you pick up the phone), negotiate as you would a car dealer. You say 240, they say 160, you say I cannot do that but pay today and I will do 220. They say 180, you say, Pay today and leave the place spotless and 200, they say OK but 190, you say 195 but you deposit the funds in my checking account at Chase (or wherever you bank) so I can avoid the PayPal fees. And they say 192.50 and you say FINE, final offer. And that's how you knock that out.

Finally for the young and broke and or otherwise...... these are tough ones. If you know you aren't going to book the weekend or especially the weekdays and people want to stay at your place very badly and they just don't have the money and they give you some of those tough luck stories like

141.

"we haven't had a vacation in 10 years, or our house just burned down, well then you can sometimes break the rules and give them a discount or even a super discount. You, again, get some cash, they get a vacation and they do usually super appreciate what you've done for them and take really good care of your place, not always, but most of the time (and that is what security deposits are for after all). I've done this from time to time and have no regrets. To me it's kind of like throwing away an old favorite sweater that doesn't fit anymore. It's really hard to throw it away, you belabor the decision but then you finally do it and three hours later you forgot you ever owned the sweater, 'out of sight out of mind' so to speak. And so it is with the property. You will not win every weekend and every stay but everything eventually comes out in the wash.

9

Establishing your contract (what to leave in, what to leave out)

As you can see a few pages on, I have included the contract that I use with my clients. Most of the contract is boilerplate; obviously you want to protect yourself and your property. If you are the super trusting type, before creating your own contract please rent the movie "Pacific Heights" a movie front the 1990's starring Michael Keaton. Long movie synopsis short it's the tale of a renter who does everything under the sun to destroy a couple of homeowners/real estate investors who are already barely scraping by, who then rent their home to a psychopath bent on bankrupting them and getting them to move out so that he and a partner can gain possession of their home.

After watching this movie sit down and being creating your document. It's a good motivator.

When I first began renting my cabin my agreement was very simple but as the years have gone by my contract has gotten more and more complex as I've dealt with varying difficulties with guests throughout the years.

What your contract should accomplish more than anything is establishing when the guest checks in and out, what can go in with them and what can leave with them when they depart, how to treat your property while they are there and lastly to protect you, your property and it's possessions while the guest is staying there. It's equally important to create a contractual agreement where you are not paying out of pocket to replace stolen or broken items. The agreement in general is that on one hand you are providing the client with a great guest experience and in return they are taking care of your property as if it were their own.

The nicer that your rental property is the more that you are going to need to protect it and the greater the array of amenities that you provide the more you are going to need to create clauses in your contract to preserve those amenities. Every aspect of your property should have clear rules and instructions for their use that are clearly posted and also laid out in your contract.

There also should be a list of repercussions in the event the rules are broken, a series of fines and levies to include but not limited to the possibility of losing their security deposit or even being removed from your property without refund.

144.

My contract

Please feel free to peruse my contract. I feel it contains most of the important language. It's still a work in progress but it should give you the basic gist. Remember that a contract should never be thought of as merely being a formality, it's a legal binding document that can save your hide in many, many situations. Also it's always super important to ensure that you have a signed contract in your hand before you let anybody walk through the door of your property. Do not, for the sake of a little short term revenue let somebody into your home with a promise that the contract is in the mail or that they will send it to you on Monday because they are checking in Friday last minute. If they truly want to rent your place they will find a Kinkos and then either fax a copy to you or sign one, scan it and e-mail it to you. The check is in the mail is the oldest trick in the book don't be fooled by it. And if something happens to your property or to them while they are there and there is no signed, completed contract you can really put yourself in a precarious or expensive situation.

Below is my contract in full:

The Cabin at Eagle Creek, A Cedarbrook East, LLC production

Rental Agreement
Please fill out (name, address, phone, total, cc#, etc.) and sign then mail to:
9740 NE Whitehorse Drive, Kingston, WA 98346

The Cabin at Eagle Creek (Cedarbrook East, LLC) is a family retreat that we share with our selected guests. We invite you to utilize all of its amenities and enjoy your vacation in the mountains! Please be respectful of the neighbors and the community, we would like to invite others to our home after your stay.

Cedarbrook East, LLC agrees to rent property located at 9820 Eagle Creek Drive, Leavenworth, Washington 98826 to _____ for the period beginning at 4 pm _____ and ending at 11 AM on _____ to no more than ___ guests.
Guest contact information: (please fill in information)
Name: _____

Names of all additional guests: (use commas)

_____

_____

_____

Employer: _____

Home Address:_____

 Home phone: _____

Work phone:_____

Cell:_____

Email: _____

1. Guests include:

Not to exceed more than 10 people at any given time; day or night. The first ten (4) people are included in the rental fee. Up to four (4) additional people are allowed with an added $20 fee per person, per day (whether or not the additional guests sleep over). The property shall not be used for any other purpose; i.e. weddings, receptions, graduation party, bachelor/bachelorette party and the like. The sole purpose of the property is for small family/friend gatherings. I have retained members of my neighborhood to keep an eye on the cabin who report disturbances to me directly. My goal is for you to enjoy your stay responsibly and to take care of my cabin as if it were your own.

3. Payment schedule:

☐   All rental fees are due immediately to hold your reservation.

☐   Balance of damage deposit (less any fees) returned within two weeks (14 days) from the end of the Term of this Agreement.

4. Confirmation:

Reservation is considered to be tentative until this contract is signed and returned to: **Cedarbrook East, LLC,** by _____ and payment received by **Kelly Kortman via check or PayPal** http://www.cabinateaglecreek.com/contact.htm

Or mailed to 9740 N.E. Whitehorse Drive, Kingston, WA Checks made payable to Kelly Kortman

5. Prices:

Rental prices will be guaranteed 120 days prior to your rental period.

6. Cancellation Policy:

Tenant may cancel this Agreement at any time prior to the beginning of the Term of this Agreement by delivering written notice of termination to Landlord (Cabin at Eagle Creek). If written notice of termination is delivered to landlord at least one hundred and twenty (120) days prior to the beginning of the Term of this agreement, Landlord shall provide full refund to the Tenant. If notice of termination is delivered to Landlord at least ninety (90) days prior to the beginning of the Term of this Agreement, Landlord shall retain $239.00 peak season/$239.00 off peak season as a non-refundable credit to be used by the tenant within one (1) year of signed agreement. If notice of termination is delivered to Landlord within thirty (30) days prior to the beginning of the Term of this Agreement, Landlord shall retain all rental funds as agreed liquidation damages for Landlord's administrative expenses and lost opportunity costs. No refund will be given due to acts of Mother Nature (lack of snowfall, rain, wind, or issues caused by such acts. i.e. .power outages, land/snow slides and so forth.)

7. Notices. Any notice in any way relating to this Agreement, or any matter arising hereunder, shall be in writing and shall be delivered by personal delivery or by U.S. mail, postage prepaid, addressed to the party to whom such notice is given at the following address or at such other address as that party notifies the other party in accordance with this Section:

To Landlord: Kelly Kortman

9740 NE Whitehorse Drive, Kingston, WA 98346

Ph: (206)992-1822 Email: kelly.kortman@gmail.com Website: www.vrbo.com/192335

To Tenant:

Name _____ Email _____

8. Damage / Noncompliance Deposit

The damage deposit shall be kept on deposit by Landlord (but need not be segregated from other of Landlord's funds) as security for any damage to the Property or any furniture, fixtures, equipment or other tangible personal property therein or disposal of garbage beyond the Waste Management garbage can provided at the rate of $10 per extra container caused by the Tenant, Tenant's guest, employees, visitors, or invitees. A $50 garbage handing fee will be added to any garbage left outside the given cans. In the event of any such damage, Landlord shall apply the damage deposit to the amount thereof. If the amount of damage exceeds the amount of the deposit, Tenant shall immediately pay the excess to Landlord. For items left behind and wanting return, a minimum $25 S&H fee will be used against the return deposit.

We feel that we rent our cabin at a very reasonable price and in exchange we ask that you take good care of our cabin, that you follow the rules and that you leave it in the condition that we ask you to leave it in. If you do not we will also charge your security deposit these various amounts for infractions.

Dishes left in sink $25 – Substantial Dog hair on couches or bedding $75 - Dog droppings left at cabin $25 – Smoking in Cabin $300 – Cigarette butts littered around cabin $50 – Late check out without permission $50 per hour – substantially filthy hot tub caused by carelessness - $50 – Miscellaneous carelessness or neglect $25-$300.

Understand we do not want to charge anybody for these infractions. When these occur however it inconveniences my cleaning staff who then has to spend additional time to rectify these situations. Please follow checkout instructions and all should be well!

We conduct a thorough inventory both prior to and after your stay. We have decorated this cabin as we would our primary residence. We would like to keep it this way and trust that our clients will leave all items in the cabin in place. Please do not remove items from the cabin as they will be charged against our damage deposit plus a restocking fee of $50.

If you invite guests into the cabin it is your responsibility as the renter to ensure that they please follow these rules to the letter. Treat this cabin as if it were your own. We appreciate you partnering with us in this effort.

Compact Discs – I make compact discs for the cabin for your enjoyment. The CD player is also IPOD compatible but there are few radio stations in the valley (although DirecTV has a number of music channels) The CD's that I make are masterpieces that I've been making for my friends for years. They take time to make, cost money to purchase the songs from I tunes or my personal music collection, cost money to deliver to the cabin and so forth. Therefore we ask that you do not take the CD's with you upon departure or even out of the cabin for that matter. There is a $35 dollar charge per disc for taking CD's from the cabin as part of the inventory process. Thank you very much for leaving them behind when you check out!

All rules and instructions in the arrival letter must be followed. These are to protect both the renting party and myself.

9. Housekeeping
Housekeeping services are not provided during the rental.

10. Property Rules:

1.   No smoking inside the building. (If you smoke outside please do not leave cigarette butts lying around, wet them in the sink and throw them in the garbage, please)
2.   Pets allowed but we must be made aware that you have a pet as we charge a pet cleaning fee.
3.   Any long distance phone calls must be collect or calling card.
4.   Guests agree to leave the property in the same general condition as they arrived
5.   All garbage must be placed in outside receptacles at the duration of the guests rental period
6.   Leave kitchen as neat as possible with dishes in the dishwasher, please run dishwasher as you head out.
7.   Quiet hours are between 12:00 AM and 9:00 AM. Please respect our neighbors.
8.   Alarm armed before leaving the house for any length of time, this is critical. We have the ability to find out when the alarm is armed and disarmed. If the cabin experiences a theft while you are staying there and the theft was due to not having set the alarm you will be held liable for the loss.

11. Right of the Landlord:
Landlord reserves and shall have the right to enter the Leased Premises at any and all times to alter, improve, repair, or add to the Building, or any part thereof, inspect the Leased Premise, or for any other purpose incident to the maintenance, conduct or operations of the Building. Tenant shall not claim, nor be allowed, any damages for any injury or inconvenience occasioned thereby. Landlord shall use reasonable care to avoid disruption of Tenant's use of the Building. This paragraph shall not in any event impose a duty on Landlord to make any repairs whatsoever.

12. Termination:
If the guest violates any of the Property Rules, which is in no way inclusive, Cedarbrook East,

LLC retains the right to terminate the guest rental agreement.

13. Holding Over:

If Tenant or any of Tenant's guests, employees, visitors or invitees fail to vacate the Property at the end of the Term of this Agreement, Tenant shall pay Landlord the sum of Five Hundred and No/100 Dollars ($500.00) for each day or portion of a day (a day being each 24 hour period from the end of the Term of this Agreement) of such failure. The preceding sentence does not give Tenant or any of its guest, employees, invitees or visitors any right to continue to occupy the Property beyond the Term of this Agreement.

14. Hold Harmless:

The guest accepts responsibility and liability for his actions and the actions of the group while s/he is in control of the property. Cedarbrook East, LLC is not responsible for acts beyond their control or for lost or stolen property and personal injury.

15. Choice of Law:

The laws of the State of Washington shall govern this rental agreement. The parties agree any action brought to enforce any provisions of this rental agreement shall be held in King County, Washington.

Cabin at Eagle Creek
9820 Eagle Creek Road ~ Leavenworth, Washington 98826

Price per day _____ x # of days _____ + misc. fees _____ +
Taxes _____ = Total or Agreed upon price_____ .

Rental Agreement

I HAVE READ IN ITS ENTIRETY ALL ATTACHED PAGES 1-3 AND
AGREE TO ABIDE BY THE TERMS 1-15 OF THIS AGREEMENT.

_____ date_____
Guest Signature
_____ *Kelly Todd Kortman*____ date _____
Owner

150.

Cancellation policy

You also want to have a clear cancellation policy. Always make it very strict, again, if something happens to your guest you can always "be cool" and offer them something that goes beyond the language of the contract but you cannot leave yourself in a situation where the guest decides to cancel a week before their stay and then wants their money back and where you are in a situation where you have no option but to give the client their money back. In this situation the client booked your place, had it reserved for them, preventing others from renting it and upon deciding it wasn't going to work out decides to get their money back with no regard for your predicament. So to prevent this I do the following:

I allow my clients to have all their money back if they cancel within 6 months of their stay, prior to three months till their stay I will allow them to cancel their reservation and use their funds within a years' time. If they cancel within 90 days of their stay I do not provide the client with any recourse. However, here is where I still try to do what I can for the client. Number one, this isn't going to happen very often but when it does I still try to provide my guests with a one year period in which to stay, the main thing that you never want to do is to pay back the money that somebody has already paid you because odds are you've either already physically or mentally spent that money.

The client needs to understand that the amount that they paid will be applied to their next stay and if those dates are more expensive or prices have risen then they are going to have to pay the difference. When I do this for clients they are typically grateful and appreciative. They might not ever stay again but they are going to walk away with a good feeling about how I've treated them.

I even had a situation once where an elderly couple came to the cabin and realized that there were more stairs than they were willing to climb up and down.

They also came out in the dead of summer and with the cabin being surrounded by grasses and trees they felt that with their slow rate of travel that they wouldn't be able to outrun a forest fire. (And really who of us can outrun a forest fire?) So upon arriving at the cabin that they had reserved for a week and had paid over a thousand dollars for they realized that they simply couldn't stay there. Of course I was waiting for the shoe to drop, for them to say that they wanted a refund. But I waited and listened and the clients were super cool. They didn't even expect a refund. Now it was true that I would have had a very difficult time trying to refund them, I did offer them the opportunity to stay at some point over the next year on a last minute or standby, space available basis. I sent them a couple of gift certificates that they could use or that they could give to somebody else and eventually that is what they did. They gave the gift certificates to their son. The son called me and asked if he could stay at a more desirable time and we were able to work out a supplemental payment in addition to the gift certificate that was going to work for both of us. Therefore we all walked away winners. Sure I could have just kept the money and I'm sure that perhaps quite a few landlords or property owners would have but that isn't me and it maybe shouldn't be you.

Later in this book we will talk about branding which by definition means, "the process involved in creating a unique name and image for a product in the consumers' mind, mainly through advertising campaigns with a consistent theme. Branding aims to establish a significant and differentiated presence in the market that attracts and retains loyal customers."

152.

When you own a small business and aren't really running advertising campaigns per se the way that you brand yourself is really by how you treat people, being consistent and providing a consistent product, gaining excellent word of mouth.

Remember that if somebody loves your property they may at best tell one or two people but if they have a terrible experience they might tell up to 5 or 10 people. So in conclusion, when dealing with clients always remember the branding element.

<u>Contracts in conclusion</u>

Finally, when dealing with guests remember that there is always a solution if you look for one. Being black and white, living by a strict set of rules, not being willing to operate in the grey area to create an excellent guest experience is only going to serve to harm you over time. Why is Nordstrom so successful? Because they don't seem to sweat the small stuff. Yes there is always going to be those people who are going to buy something, wear it, return it and try to get their money back with malice aforethought. But the 98% who shop with you because of your liberal and agreeable return policy and who rarely return stuff are going to more than make up for those greedy and careless few.

10

Additional Financial Benefits

<u>Tax Benefits of Owning a Rental Property</u>

Owning a rental property may be one of the better tax shelters that still exists. There is so much that you can deduct when you own a rental property. First and foremost you get to deduct the mortgage interest. I have a primary residence and I have my rental property. My total monthly mortgage payments are pretty substantial and I get to write the vast majority of that off of my income. In addition to that you may be able to depreciate the property itself and all the possessions within.

Also, every year you are going to have both property expenses and business expenses.

Some of these might include but aren't limited to the cost of supplies, the cost of replacing worn out equipment or maintaining equipment. For example in the last two years alone I had to replace a washing machine, a mini fridge (where I keep some of my personal items either cold or frozen) and a garbage disposal. In the fall of last year I finally caved in and decided to have my deck completely rebuilt after spending years patching it up over and over again. I also just got to a point where I wanted to update my fridge and stove from white to stainless steel. In doing all of these things I'm forever improving my property and making it more rentable yes but I'm also potentially helping to reduce my tax liability over time by creating tax write-offs, in this case creating a series of expenses that can be depreciated.

Yes, it is never pleasant when you have to spend good money to replace these things but it's a necessary evil to keep your place up and running at all times and you do eventually get some of that money back when you file your return.

Real Estate Professional

One of the biggest benefits of owning a rental property though is if you are running the place yourself and especially if you are spending 750 hours a year working as what the IRS calls a "real estate professional". Now you might think that it would be hard to get to 750 hours a year running your property but you would be wrong. I usually end up at my cabin about every two months. When I'm there I almost always spend a good solid day or two doing maintenance and cleaning.

Even though you have a cleaner who is conducting your cleans for you - you are still going to have those big project that come up from time to time. Whether that is the big spring clean up, clearing brush, landscaping, painting or blacktopping your driveway there is always going to be things that need to be done with your property (In fact I've yet to go to my property when there wasn't some form of work that needed to be done.)

Every cleaner is different but odds are your cleaner is probably not going to be super interested in weeding, raking, draining and filling the hot tub, pressure spraying the driveway and doing a host of other things that you as a meticulous property owner are going to want to see done and if you want to be successful you are going to need to be meticulous. So if you plan on making it to your cabin about 6 times a year for 2 days at a time and spend 8 hours working on your place per day then that is 96 hours right there. Then every spring and fall I typically go out and put in a full week of painting and cleaning and maintenance. This April for example I put in a solid 70 hours in one week doing all of the necessary work.

So having done all that I was now at 160 plus hours, only 600 more to go. With 365 days in the year divided by the remaining 600 hours you only need to put in about an hour and a half a day to get you the rest of the way. Now on some days of course you won't have anything to do at all, on other days, when you are dealing with multiple guest inquiries, dealing with a current client issue, handling payments or getting your calendar up to speed it can turn out to be much more than that. I do find that there is usually something to do every day whether it be responding to inquiries, dealing with guests and bookings, paying cabin bills, coordinating with your cleaner, updating your VRBO site, updating your calendar, the list goes on and on and sooner or later you will find that "voila", you have achieved the 750 hour requirement.

Once you've achieved that requirement you are going to be able to write off any and all passive real estate losses, not a portion thereof. A passive loss is any loss incurred through a rental property and can be used to offset the passive income that you earn from your rental property. A passive loss cannot be written off against income from your job. If you are a higher wage earner (and typically most people with vacation properties are higher income earners, especially in the day and age of super stringent underwriting standards) and not a real estate professional you would not be able to write off your passive real estate losses in its entirety or at all depending on how much money that you make. But if you are a real estate professional then you most likely can.

This fact in and of itself is reason alone to take care of all of these cabin responsibilities yourself. I would find out that in 2012 alone, if I had not put in the hours to qualify as a real estate professional that my income tax liability would have been some $32,000 dollars more. So when you take that dollar amount into consideration along with all that you save being a "do it yourselfer" you can see the value add of putting in the time to become a "real estate professional."

I'd also like to add here that I didn't create the tax code but I sure am going to take every single allowable deduction and work within the confines of the system to pay not a penny more than I have to.

I believe that when you start renting out your vacation property you in effect become a small business owner. You are taking risks that every other American could they themselves take. Starting a business is a very risky proposition; you are putting your hard earned money in the form of working capital to get your business started. You deserve to pay less in taxes as you get your business off the ground. And just like every small business owner who hit it big you have a chance to generate tons of revenue and therefore tax dollars for the government down the road.

And if you hit it big you are going to need employees who in turn will be paying taxes of their own. It might seem like a quirky, complex system but it works and has fueled a thousand success stories over time making America the land of opportunity that it still remains today.

Lastly, running your own business may allow you to deduct any or all of the costs of running that business to include any equipment that you are going to need to own to run that business. Computers, printers, cell phone, home phone, office space in your home, automobile expenses related to your business, gasoline, travel time, marketing and advertising. All of these things are deductible in one way, shape or form and it's important that you hire an excellent CPA in your area who understands the term "real estate professional" and who can ensure that you are getting every tax break that you deserve.

The three year rule

Most businesses are not going to be profitable for the first three years that you own them. First of all there are going to be fairly large startup costs that you have to recoup before you can consider yourself profitable.

If you own a vacation rental because you wanted to own a vacation rental and then later decided that you either wanted or needed the cash flow from the vacation rental then you have a huge leg up. First and foremost you can clearly afford the mortgage and the expenses of running a second home. Otherwise you wouldn't own the property in the first place. It's also fairly safe to assume that your place is already furnished. Even if it's not furnished in such a way that would compel people to want to pay a high price to stay there yet, it might also be safe to assume that you still have a big head start over somebody who is going to purchase a place from scratch and therefore have to fully furnish it.

158.

Perhaps you just need to go out and purchase a few things. In this case, where you already own the property and have furnished it, then you are going to be profitable in the month that you bring in more in one month than you are paying out in mortgage payments and expenses. Had I taken over my cabin earlier in the game I might have been profitable earlier as well. I did find that I really started to become quite profitable around 2010. By this point I had had my property in the VRBO for quite some time and I had really gained a knack for keeping the place rented all the time through my various aforementioned pricing strategies and so forth. I feel that with this book you will also have a much better chance of being profitable sooner than that. It all depends on your rate of learning and ability to acclimate and apply what you are learning here and most importantly finding the things that work for you.

Economics 101 and real estate as an investment

Having been a financial advisor for the last 12 years I've come to understand a great many things. I'm not going to go into too great of detail as this isn't a crash course in economics but I feel that there are a few important things to understand.

The most important thing that I've learned as it pertains to real estate is that the stock market and the real estate market seem to follow each other somewhat closely. The stock market can sometimes decline because real estate is performing poorly or sometimes it seems that the real estate market can perform badly because the stock market is performing poorly. Everything is intertwined and somewhat meshed together.

159.

The stock market going down could mean a current or future bad economy and a bad economy could result in higher unemployment and higher unemployment could mean that the real estate market takes a hit as we head into a period of foreclosures.

Conversely a strong real estate market can sometimes do wonders for the economy and thus the stock market (something that we may be experiencing now as I write this in 2013). The theory goes something like this. During a recovery the stock market usually recovers first. This is because the "smart money" is out there buying stocks at cheap prices in hopes or in belief that a recovery is on its way (as has happened every single time thus far when we've had an economic calamity). The next thing to recover is usually corporate earnings as people start spending money again. As spending increases manufacturing has to increase to meet demand and therefore people have to be hired to be able to facilitate rising manufacturing. As this happens unemployment declines and sooner or later these now employed people are going to need housing. As people purchase this new housing they need to furnish it, purchase appliances and other dry goods, sometimes they have kids and as they do spending increases yet again and before you know it you are in a full blown economic recovery. As the demand for housing begins to outstrip the current housing supply housing prices typically rise. It's simple and yet it's complex and of course anything can happen at any time to stop a recovery in its tracks (rising interest rates, war, etc.)

In fact here are a few charts that illustrate just how closely they can follow each other, sometimes on a 12 month lag and sometimes more concurrently.

Here is a microcosm chart of New York City Real Estate vs. the Dow Jones Industrial Average:

160.

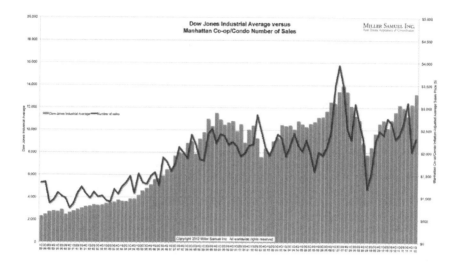

Here is another chart showing a long term chart of the housing market vs. the stock market in general:

The charts on the preceding page does illustrate that there is definitely a high correlation; however, the stock market historically clearly outperforms real estate over the long haul.

Patience is rewarded both in the stock market and the real estate market. Obviously it's much easier to be patient in the real estate market than it is in the stock market because oftentimes you either need to have a house to live in or if you own a rental property the rent checks that you are receiving are going to be much more important to you than what the current appraised value of that property currently is.

We often say in my business that people are lucky that they don't get a monthly statement telling them what their home is worth because if they did a good percentage of them would sell their homes after a few down statements. Human nature or emotions many times creates situations where people love to buy things at the worst time possible and then sell them again at the worst time possible. Whether it's stocks, bonds, real estate, gold or oil futures. The masses have a tendency to jump on the bandwagon at the very tail end of the mania and those folks typically end up holding the bag as the whole thing implodes on itself. Although people typically buy their first home when they need housing and are tired of making rent payments (which can happen at any time during an economic cycle) people who invest in second homes typically do it because everybody is currently talking about what an awesome time it is to buy real estate (which ironically is usually the worst time to buy real estate!)

There is a always a bubble to invest in somewhere and there are those who always seem to invest in that bubble at its peak, whether it was the technology stock bubble of 1998-2000, the oil bubble of 2006-2008, the gold bubble of 2005-2011 or the real estate bubble of 2004-2007.

People have a hard time buying investments when they are unloved (where were all the gold buyers when it was at $400 an ounce in 2005?) and they also have a hard time selling the investments that they own which have done really well and which might possibly have topped out and these are the things that wreak havoc on people's portfolios. There is no question that I have very successful clients and I have those who have not fared as well and it has nothing to do most times with the stock market or timing but has everything to do with their emotions towards the market. My successful clients by and large just seem to peacefully understand that they are in the market for the long run while others are constantly trying to time the market and are constantly going through these greed/fear cycles. I find it interesting as well that my well off clients are the more passive types while my less well off clients are more likely to get sucked into the greed/fear cycle patterns. They are also more likely to want to invest in stock and real estate market bubbles. They are also apt to come in and ask me if they should invest in this or that at the top of that market's bubble.

My takeaway from this is that if you are wanting to invest in real estate mainly for the price appreciation of that property and if you know in your heart that you are susceptible to investing in markets at the wrong time or if you have ever said to yourself that "the stock market is a rigged game" then you probably might not be a great candidate for real estate investment either.

What I've also learned is that since the market became regulated in the mid 1930's the market has seemingly traveled in a somewhat predictable cycle. Maybe not to the point where you can set your watch to what you think it might do next but possibly close. Since the 1930's, after the market was regulated, we've seen a pattern of very rare, yet periodic 50% declines in the market that seem to happen about every 35 years.

163.

This is typically followed by a 6 year recovery pattern as the stock market works to move back up to a point where it was prior to the crash. Best of all this has historically been followed by a 20 year bull market which has typically taken the market up by up to 10 times or even more. Lastly, this is usually followed by a 10 or so year period of uncertainty. Based on this observation I've made (Nobody ever brought this to my attention) there is as chance that we might possibly be in the first year of a 20 year bull market.

I mean I certainly cannot promise that and anything can happen but if there is one thing that I do know it's that history has a tendency to repeat itself, that the stock market goes up over the long haul as a result of population growth and inflation (more people buying more products at higher prices over time leading to higher corporate profits and therefore higher share prices). All of the rest of the 'white noise' out there, i.e. the 24 hour news cycle, who our current president is, wars and rumors of wars all of those things though temporarily impactful and typically difficult to trade around (especially with real estate due to its relative illiquidity in times of crisis) are nothing more than chatter that just distracts us from getting to where we should get over time with our investments.

So what methods can you employ to be successful in any market? Patience, investing for the long run, being diversified, turning off the nightly news and trying to understand the long term charts to make long term financial decisions. You know who does really well in the stock market? Warren Buffet. And last I checked the guy was doing pretty darn well. In fact most every successful investor from Buffett to Peter Lynch to Sir John Templeton all believed in the same thing, that you buy great companies at cheap prices and you hold them for a long time or until they fully recover, whichever seems to come first. This is why the "Dogs of the Dow" theory seems to work pretty well.

164.

It's merely a strategy where you buy the 5 worst performing stocks in the DOW Jones Industrial average and hold them until they've recovered. You know who didn't believe in that? Gordon Gekko and if I recall correctly at the end of Wall Street he ended up in jail.

Below is a chart of the stock market since 1900, if you take one thing away from this simply take away that since the bottom of the market in 1933 the market has risen from 45 to 14,500 despite a half dozen wars both hot and cold, a host of regional economic collapses and enough depressing stories on the nightly news to fill up the entire universe. The one thing that I've also learned is that it's going to be hard to believe the hype if you aren't listening to it.

(apologies if this chart is too small in the current print format, but this chart is easily found online by googling "stock market 1900-present")

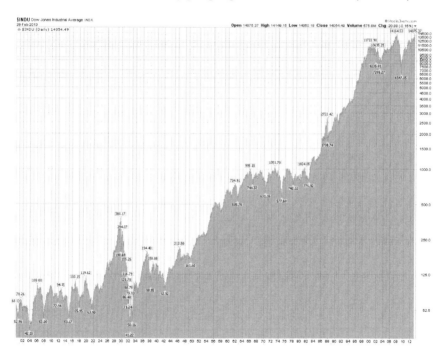

165.

If we are right now in the first year of a 20 year bull market that is going to potentially bode quite well for anybody purchasing real estate today. And of course when would have been the best time to buy real estate? Probably in 2009 or 2010 when nobody really wanted to buy anything and everybody was hunkering down and waiting for Armageddon (which although predicted a hundred times throughout history has yet to show make its presence felt just yet). However, in looking out over the long run and while taking into consideration where real estate has been and where I think it's going I do believe that now could be a good time to jump in. Although interest rates have moved up they are still very low historically speaking. I'm of the opinion that we might not see interest rates as low as they recently were for a very long time to come, but, that is mere speculation. Real estate in many parts is still much less expensive than it was in 2006 so there is value in that I believe also. People are absolutely traveling again and spending money and a lot of the fear we saw in the market in 2009 seems to have been erased. People do seem more hopeful about the near future and that is a good thing as well. There are some nagging issues that remain and might always be with us; global warming, some lingering pain in the job market, economic issues in Europe and a handful of other sticking points. The thing to remember is that there are ALWAYS going to be issues. In the 1910's it was probably World War I. In the 1920's many felt the world was in a moral decline, there was a lot of corruption and gangster activity, there was the great depression in the 1930's, World War II in the 1940's, the Cold War began in the 1950's. All of these things seemed insurmountable at the time and yet we worked our way through every single one of them. It was also believe that by the year 2000 there wouldn't be a single tree left at the current rate of consumption in the mid twentieth century and we found a solution for that as well. It does seem that we always prevail and that science and technological advances eventually win the day. I'm optimistic that we will yet find a solution to our current issues and if we do then things can really take off!

166.

10

Troubleshooting client issues

Inevitably you are going to have client issues large and small; there is no two ways about it. There are a million things that you can do to prevent them, and you should, but all the preparation and planning in the world is not going to help to prevent the occasional dilemma.

Owning a cabin is kind of like selling an IKEA dining set. You can sell it at a fair price and you can provide an excellent set of instructions on how to put it together but that isn't going to guarantee that somebody isn't going to try to return that table having glued the chair legs to the table and the table legs to the chairs. So first off I'm going to reiterate some things that will help you to avoid a lot of the problems you can end up facing, then I will walk you through how to resolve them.

Double bookings

Sooner or later you are going to have a double booking. It's one of the most painful things that you are going to face as a vacation rental owner. They are costly, time consuming and are a horrible experience for both you and the guests and that typically includes both renting parties, meaning the party that got to your rental first and the one who got there second.

The way to avoid them is to update your calendar immediately upon booking your property. This can be hard to do all the time because of our very busy lives but if you do this then you are going to avoid a lot of heartache. Trust me; I've learned the hard way. When I get behind in moving bookings to my calendar I try to do some of the following things. I always make the client email me with their request to stay and again, I create a fresh email with the title "cabin at eagle creek". This way I can run a search in Gmail and I can pull up all the email requests to stay and match those against my calendar, if all of those bookings are in and there are no double bookings, I'm good. Sometimes people are not internet savvy and they want to communicate by phone. That is fine but in that case you should *e-mail yourself,* put VRBO or the name of your property in the "subject field" and include the client's name, phone number and desired dates. This way you can keep tabs on the client, not forget about the client and be able to conduct a search for prospective or locked in upcoming guests.

If you are taking payments primarily through PayPal (like I am with my "buy now" button) then it's quite easy to run a search through there also to see when a client paid, how much they've paid and so forth. Those payments are also going to show up in your email if your PayPal is set up to send you email updates when payments are received or when money is moved to your checking account.

<u>Whiteboard</u>

The other thing that I do is I have a whiteboard at home with a big calendar on it, I also have the next four months in the blank area to the left as illustrated below.

The main part of the whiteboard has the month we are currently in. Most often by the time that I've gotten to that month that month is already pretty heavily booked, but it is nice to have a visual of that calendar. I also have somewhat of a "photographic" memory.

I understand that not everybody has this but I can almost recall in my mind's eye which days are still available and which are not.

This is another way that I can quickly write in names that I know that I've booked so I have both a mental image of my calendar and so that I can quickly write down new guests names so that I can add them to my calendar later. Therefore sometimes it's a matter of moving names from the whiteboard to my VRBO calendar and sometimes it's a matter of moving them from my calendar to my whiteboard but I do know this; If my whiteboard and calendar are perfectly aligned then I know that my calendars are up to date and in good order and if I have no double bookings then I'm in great shape.

Another way that I keep my calendar up to date is to sporadically go through my contracts and ensure that for every contract that I have there is a booking on the calendar. I keep all my active contracts in a folder and I go through them from time to time ensuring two things, one being that all "old contracts" meaning everybody who has already checking out, that I've permanently filed away that contract. Then I go through what is left and ensure that for everybody who is staying over the next couple of weeks that I have their contract. If I don't I remind them via email to get it into me. I've found some missed bookings that way also.

It's also important to do this so that your calendar matches your contracts. If you have bookings in your calendar and no contract then you obviously need to get that before guests check into your cabin. Not that anyone might abuse that but technically they can move in and squat as they are not contractually obligated to check out! And with no security deposit you are totally at risk and the guest has no skin in the game if something goes wrong, something is broken or something is stolen during the course of their stay.

One last point on this, if the client has failed to send in their contract and a double booking does occur then they really don't have much recourse because really without having sent me the signed contract they don't have any rights to the cabin. Of course I'm going to refund their money, however, I spell it out very clearly that the client is going to need to sign and send in the contract. The contract is what makes the vacation rental business world go around. So no contract, again, no rights.

Something that might also come in handy might be to simply pin the contract to the bottom of your whiteboard (my whiteboard has a little corkboard near the bottom of it just like the one on the previous page). This way if you have two contracts pinned up for the same weekend you know right away if you have a double booking or not. Another way to go about this is simply using a variety of checkmarks letting you know that a certain booking written onto your whiteboard has paid, has sent in their contract and has provided a security deposit.

<u>Providing door codes just prior to client stay</u>

I also usually do not provide door codes until just a few days before a client's stay. This way I know right away if a guest is asking for a code but I don't have them on the calendar.

Double bookings, as bad as they are - are made even worse when two guests actually show up at the cabin. This happens when you've completely spaced that a guest has booked and paid for a certain period of dates. At this point you can still provide a refund and help the client to find alternative accommodations.

It's also important to scan through the contract to ensure that people haven't crossed anything out and initialed it.

171.

If they don't agree to something in your contract there is a chance that you can come to terms with them about whatever the issue might be that concerns them. But you don't want to wake up one day and find out that the client crossed out the part of the contract that refers to not allowing pets in the hot tub or some other critical portion.

Doing the right thing

Now most times by doing the above things you will avoid a double booking. If you do catch the error prior to the guests staying you have to immediately call the guest who booked second (not the guest who paid you the lesser amount of money or who agreed to stay for the shorter period of days...) and let them know there has been a mistake. These people are not going to be happy but you have to refund their money immediately and you should help them to find a like place as quickly as possible and then on top of that you should offer them a free night in the future. When it becomes so late that a guest has paid you already and they are at your doorstep then it might just make sense to find them equal or better accommodations and pay for their stay out of pocket. It's important to let the client know that they can either have their money back or that you will find them an equal or better place and simply pay for it. (While trying to remember to ensure the client jumps back in to cover their own security deposit). It's also important to point out that you aren't both providing them a refund and purchasing a place for them to stay as well. I had a client get confused about that once with me and insisted that I said that I was going to do both. Nobody in their right mind in business would ever agree to that but still, that said, by letting the client not only know what you will do but what you *won't do,* can be very wise and cost effective.

The thing about people's vacations is that they start to visualize their vacation in advance of their stay. When you call them to cancel their reservation all of those dreams go up in smoke and at that point the client will be brimming with disillusionment.

172.

It can even sometimes make sense to find them a slightly better location and pay the difference. In this business your reputation is everything so you have to make things right or even better than right. And fast. It is important to note that a guest can only leave a comment if they actually stayed at your vacation rental. So luckily if you do have issues perhaps negotiating with a guest or even have a double booking the guest who arrived second and was provided a refund and a few options of where else they might be able to stay cannot leave a nasty comment on your VRBO comments site; on Yelp, yes, they can, but in the critical VRBO comments section, no, they cannot and that is an important point of note.

The best case scenario that can result from this situation is when you can get one of the guests to move their dates ahead or back a week. This is only accomplished if you catch the double booking sometimes days but more often weeks in advance. At this point you can offer them some free weekdays or offer up some other type of benefit to encourage them to be flexible. Kind of like when they overbook an airline, they will let you fly on the next flight and give you a cash voucher for free travel in the future and for the travelers who can be flexible it's a real win/win. The airline isn't losing anything because most flights do not go out completely full and the traveler gets a nice little free trip at some point down the road.

Oftentimes this soothes the client and un-ruffles the feathers and everybody can move on with their lives. You might be a little lighter in the pocketbook but tragedy averted.

Getting a client rebooked

Now, if you actually end up with a double booking where you have both guests at the cabin at the same time, well, it's pretty much the same process but you also have to deal with clients who are currently freaking out and feeling homeless.

173.

If they have elderly people with them or small children or if it's a hundred degrees out or people have food spoiling in their car then it's even worse. People get panicky and start having heat flashes and fits of denial and anger. Once the client is done venting (and don't let them go on for more than a few minutes) calmly diffuse the situation by letting them know that come hell or high water everything will be fixed.

You've already made money that weekend because clearly you already have somebody in your cabin. You might have to end up spending a little bit of that money to make things right but remember, since you already have that client's revenue in your bank account you are really going to be using *their* funds to rebook them.

Therefore the first thing you have to do is immediately let them know that you are going to take care of everything. What I have normally done in these situations is let the person who got their first and who has probably already settled in, unpacked, filled up the fridge and perhaps already taken a shower or a nap, stay. The person who showed up second I will immediately find accommodations for.

Develop a roster of "go to" properties

First and foremost it's important to have a roster of like properties in your area or to even create strategic partnerships so that you can send your overflow to them and vice versa. (Truth be told getting a surprise booking for an empty weekend last minute from one of these strategic partnerships is really nothing more than pennies from heaven.)

It's also important to find a property manager in the area who manages an entire pool of properties. Most vacation towns have them. I used to be in one as I mentioned prior to running my place independently.

Because they run this pool of properties a few likelihoods result. One, you are going to get a hold of a human being immediately and they are going to have something that is usually going to work for the client. They can usually book the place right away and take your credit card over the phone. You typically, again, just keep the revenue from the client and then pay for them to stay at the other location. The bad news is that those places are usually going to gouge you because they know you are in a desperate situation. So the best bet is to contact these types of establishments and develop a relationship with the owner on the front end as mentioned earlier. The very best thing you can do is to pre-negotiate a percentage discount because you are, after all, providing them with business; this business is usually last minute business for places that would have otherwise gone unrented. These places also don't care about attaining top dollar because they make money regardless and then send a small amount of revenue to the owner of the property themselves. Best bet though is to find a place on the VRBO first although it's likely you aren't going to have time to do it because the client is going to need action now. Murphy's Law also dictates that the double booking will happen on one of the busiest days of the year like Labor Day or something like that so finding a like property is going to be like Joseph and Mary finding a room at the Inn. The more demand there is for a particular weekend the more likely you are to double book it, it's that simple. Almost all of my double bookings so far have been on Labor Day or Memorial Day weekend. This is also usually a time when finding a property is like pulling teeth. I've luckily, however, always managed to make this happen thus far. Then again, I consider myself to be very resourceful. After doing this a few times you will be certain that you could absolutely do a fine job in hostage negotiating. I'm not kidding.

Once you have gotten the client settled in be sure to call the client in your home and apologize for the inconvenience, they are probably going to be a little bit stressed as well.

175.

The thing that can occur also is they are both going to have the code to gain entry. I've only had about three double bookings in the last 5 years (despite how experienced I might sound in dealing with these happenstances) but on two occasions the second party to arrive was very testy with the party that arrived first. I've even had them confront the first party to arrive to prove that they had the right to be there. I've had the second party actually burst through the door and demand to walk around the cabin as if they were in disbelief that this was happening to them. Again it can be unsettling.

One other thing that I've done is create a relationship and a credit in town with a small local winery. Whenever I've had an inconvenience of this nature I've also been sure to get the inconvenienced guest a bottle of wine. For $10 or $15 bucks you at the very least show the client your concern. It goes a long way. Wine for some reason seems to be the great soother and the gift that keeps on giving. This I believe goes back to the story of Jesus at the wedding, everybody loves a nice glass of wine now and again, especially when it's seemingly run out.

Damage to your property

Over time, just like with double bookings, you are going to have damage to your property. It's a fact of life. Things break when you are at home all the time and it's safe to assume that it's going to happen to your cabin as well.

Most times clients will call to tell you they broke something or sometimes actually they call you to tell you that something is broken. Either way if it occurred under their watch then it's your turn to decide whether the breakage was intentional or on accident. Then you need to determine the probable cost of repair and then you need to decide whether to chalk it up to the "cost of doing business" or to make the client pay for it out of their security deposit.

176.

The worst experience to date

It's never going to be fun to find that your property has experienced damage. It can get even trickier when you find out about damage having occurred while your guests are still at your property. What you are about to read is a true story which represents one of the worst ownership experiences that I've ever had. Now I know that this story probably pales in comparison to those who rent their properties out to people for months or years but this, for me, is as bad as it's been so far, but also how I was able to reconcile the situation.

To begin, I had 5 women staying at my cabin, a grandmother, a mother and their three female daughters. There were immediate problems out of the gate. First and foremost they were very difficult to book. They kept delaying making the payment even after several promises that they would do it no later than the next morning. But it kept not getting done. Then I would come to later realize that in all of the drama in trying to secure the payment that they had never sent me a security deposit or a signed contract. Mistake number one, I didn't go through my contracts and verify through my calendar who sent in what. Guests are tricky.

They will sometimes send you only a part of the contract back, they will sign it in the wrong place, they will leave out important information in the blanks of your boilerplate contract. Once again, it's important to go through the contract and make sure that it's in good order. If you don't, again, you can be left vulnerable. Additionally as a convenience to both myself and the client I do not deposit security deposit checks into my account unless if something goes wrong. This way I save a step in that I don't have to then pull the funds back out and send them back to the client. But I guess this could leave me vulnerable as well if a client decided to put a stop payment on a check.

177.

However, in the past I've usually gone in and deposited the check and *then* told the client that I had to do that because of damage to the property. 99% of the time you aren't going to have to worry about these types of situations but when they do happen they seem to happen in the worst way possible.

Next, upon arriving at the cabin these 5 women tried to turn on the cabin lighting outside (Christmas lights) but the previous guest had blown a fuse in the plug of the Christmas lights so they weren't working and I hadn't had a chance to go out and fix them yet. So they found this troubling and called me about it. I explained the situation and they were OK with it but, you know, not thrilled. I mean I love Christmas lights as much as anybody but we were only in like the first week of December and there was plenty of Christmas atmosphere to go around with snow falling heavily around the property.

One evening while the kids were outside in the hot tub they decided to try to figure out how to get the Christmas lights to work on their own and while they were trying to plug the lights in or get them to work they ended up shutting off the spa at the breaker. Even though it's in the contract, arrival letter and written on the plastic cover of the breaker not to touch it unless of emergency the teenage kids went ahead and opened that box and tried to turn on the Christmas lights through the spa breaker. So through the night the spa started to cool and, as you might understand, in the middle of winter a spa that's been turned off can freeze wreaking havoc on your pumps, heaters and pipes.

Later the clients called me to say that the spa wasn't working. So after trying to troubleshoot the situation over the phone with no luck we had no choice but to call an electrician to and rectify the situation. (While he was there I should have had him fix my Christmas lights also considering the price he charged but I had forgotten about that).

178.

While speaking to the electrician on the phone, even though he admitted that he was going to have to drive past my cabin on his way home anyway, he still charged me $75 for his services. That's right - $75 - to flip a switch.

When the electrician came out and we realized that the kids had turned off the breaker I very gently told the clients that they were going to be on the hook for that $75. The client immediately became defensive and started to expound as to why she wasn't going to be paying that amount. I very calmly stated that she wasn't going to have to pay me per se as it would be coming out of the security deposit. To which she replied, "What security deposit?" We never gave you a security deposit. This was when I realized that I had no contract and no security deposit and was in fact a serious victim of Murphy's Law.

The one time you have damage to your property that is provable and significant you don't have a contract or anything else for that matter to keep the situation fair and the guests honest. For a moment there our conversation became a bit tenuous. I was basically telling the guest that we were going to have to come up with some way for her to cover the loss and she was saying that she wasn't going to pay me anything. She was generally trying to turn things around to somehow suggest that everything and anything that occurred had to have been my fault or basically trying to point out anything that she could that was a negative about my property in an effort to say that somehow we surely must be even.

It was at this point that I simply let the client know that she had me over a barrel. That yes, she could basically walk away from the situation Scott free because I had failed to secure a contract or a security deposit. But I then said, "Ma'am, I think you know what the right thing to do here is. You know and I know that that breaker shouldn't have been turned off. But it was, and having turned off the breaker cost me $75. I then asked her to 'put herself in my shoes'.

179.

I asked her, "What if you were trying to run a business and somebody hurt your business financially, even if it was an accident, you would expect them to step up and take care of the situation correct?"

I went on to say," Now I cannot tell you what to do and I cannot make you do anything here, but it's my hope that you will do the right thing." In saying this it was my hope that the client would step up and send me a check for the $75 bucks. Yes they had paid me a fair amount of money to stay at my cabin during one of the highest weekends of the year, but you have to remember that the point of being in business is to make a profit and you will never be profitable if you are simply giving things away.

As it was the clients checked out the next day. And that next day around evening time the client called me to say that in addition to everything else that had gone wrong that they had also blown out all of the glass on my fireplace doors as a result of having built too large of a fire and when the logs settled one of them fell against the glass and before they could do anything about the burning log it just heated and then exploded glass and ash all over my living room, having had this happen before I knew that this was going to be yet another $400 to fix. I mean we were now coming to a point where half or more of the money that they had paid me to merely rent the place wasn't even going to be enough to cover my damages.

I once again pleaded my case with the client. I explained to her that what she had paid was a fair price to rent my cabin for that weekend. That obviously I take huge pride in my place and I got her to quickly agree that when she checked in the place was spotless, beautiful and completely working and functional. I then explained to her that only a few times a year do we ever have anything ever break and that that weekend alone she had broken or corrupted two very significant things.

180.

I also explained that if major breakage like this happened EVERY weekend I would have gone into foreclosure years ago and that the rental income that I, in fact, do receive is the income that I need to make my mortgage payment.

The one ace that I knew that I had in my pocket was small claims court. Even though I didn't have a signed contract I still had the right to take our situation before a judge. Small claims court is an annoyance for everybody. Having to go to small claims is never fun and it pretty much means an entire day off of work and if she, as the defendant, had lost she would have had to pay me for the damages plus my court costs and if she didn't pay then she could get a county court judgment against her. I did not want to use this particular ace in the hole so I tried another tactic.

Contractually she wasn't obligated to do anything but I appealed to her higher sense of decency and asked her if she would be willing to pay for half of the damages or around $230 dollars. She did agree to do just that and the end result was as follows: the weekend still turned a profit, an electrician made $75 for 10 minutes of work thus stimulating the Leavenworth economy and I got newer and higher quality fireplace doors (ceramic glass as opposed to tempered which took my rating to 1500 degrees as opposed to 500 degrees) that hopefully won't break again under any conditions.

The lesson I learned here is that you have to ensure that you have your ducks in a row with each client. I will do whatever it takes to not let this happen to me again. I also learned a few things about diplomacy and appealing to a guest's sense of what is right. They are after all staying in your home for a fee and common decency should always reign supreme above all other things.

I also learned that half of something is way better than all of nothing and I found a way to get a portion of what I deserved without resorting to court.

If she had not agreed to pay anything I would have taken her to small claims court and I'm fairly certain I would have won unless if she had the audacity to lie to a judge but I will say that she didn't seem the type.

In conclusion, when you have damage it's always going to be a judgment call. Things do break after all, normally it's called "planned obsolescence" I mean not everything can be designed to last forever, not even plastic, but some things can be purchased that are going to last a lot longer than so many other types of things. It's really about determining whether the breakage was due to negligence or accident. You really should never charge a client for something that was broken on accident. You might also be surprised by the fact that when people break things, if they have a conscience, they will usually step up and offer to pay for it. Sometimes things just so happen to finally fail when your guests are staying at your property. If your microwave suddenly stops working for example it's going to be super hard to prove that the guest broke your microwave and odds are they didn't. It just happened on their watch. However, if all your plates are broken and you know for a fact that a Greek wedding was just performed at your property there is probably a pretty good chance that that party is responsible and that you should probably charge the damages against their security deposit.

One last comment about guest reviews on VRBO and the importance thereof. You really want to proceed cautiously when keeping a guests security deposit. One bad comment on your vrbo probably won't kill you but two might certainly have a very negative impact. It tells the client that there is a chance that something might go wrong. A quick example of this is that I stayed at a really nice place on the North Shore of Hawaii.

182.

Upon arrival to this property we were very pleased, it was well appointed and modern and in a decent enough area. If we had any problem with the place it was that one bedroom had A/C and the other one did not. I mean, really, one person gets A/C and the other person gets to suffer?

Also the pictures of the place made the house seem as though it was right on the beach and a sandy beach no less. As it turned out the place was not on a beach but a block from it and the beach wasn't sandy at all in fact it was straight up lava beds and tide pools, very neat but not very cozy to lay on. However, I recently went back to the VRBO about possibly renting this property again and as fate would have it this residence now has two very bad reviews, one because of a double booking where it appears that the owner didn't step up quite enough to help the guests (this is Hawaii after all and people are flying in from all around the world making even the smallest inconvenience much bigger). The other bad review was seemingly the result of the guest taking out the rental's bicycles for the day (yes, this particular rental came with 2 beach cruisers) and then having been unfortunate enough to have had those bicycles stolen. The owner, probably doing the right thing kept the security deposit and used it to by new bicycles but the guests then, of course, left a scathing review. Now this review in and of itself probably wouldn't have been the death knell. It's also true that as an owner you have a chance to respond to all your reviews. You do not, however, have an opportunity to really dispute the review unless you have incontrovertible evidence that the guest is lying. So as long as the guest has stayed at your property they have the right to leave a review and there is little you can do to have that review removed.

Again, it's really the combination of several bad reviews that kind of crush you even if all the other reviews are good. It just leaves that nagging doubt in a guest's mind.

183.

And considering that this is a numbers game, even if you lose out on one or two bookings a month you are talking about forgoing up to eighteen thousand dollars a year in revenue. So at this point you have to ask yourself, is keeping one security deposit of $300 worth losing out on $18,000 dollars every year in future revenue? Here are a few more problems that you might have with guests.

Excessive noise

I'm lucky in that my cabin is fairly isolated from my neighbors (you might wish to find the same, people on vacation like to drink, play cards, listen to music and be loud) and in five years I've never had a noise complaint. However, if you ever do you can count on receiving that awful phone call in the middle of the night usually. The key here is to give the clients one opportunity to be quiet and to let them know that if they have yet another noise complaint that odds are the next people to be called is not going to be you but probably the police and that if the police are called and end up at the property that they are going to lose their security deposit and possibly be removed from your property. One thing that you can also probably expect is that where there is noise there is also possibly going to be damage; after all it's not a party until something gets broken, right?

It sometimes feels harsh when you have to lay down the law but the last thing you want is your neighbors hating you. Remember that you are going to be staying at your property from time to time or even quite often and the surest way to have neighbors who do not like you is to continually have problems with noisy guests. It's also my recommendation that if you do have to withhold a portion of the security deposit (and this is something you want written into their contract so contractually the guests have to oblige and understand how your series of fines are going to work)

184.

you should use some of that money to do something nice for the neighbors whether that is a bottle of wine or a cake or a trip to a spa depending on how badly the neighbors currently want you to sell your property never to return.

Place left excessively messy, rules not followed or late checkouts

Messy houses, unfollowed rules, broken items; all of these things are going to inconvenience your cleaning staff and are going to be costly to you. The best route to go in these cases is to have your cleaner send you an email with their findings once they've finished doing their clean. If cleaning staff have to leave and come back because the guests cannot seem to get out of bed, pack their suitcase and get into their car then your cleaner is going to have to leave and come back and they are usually going to charge you for their lost time, if it takes them an extra hour to clean they are going to charge you for that also. It also is important for the cleaner to take a camera phone shot of the most egregious part of whatever they left behind so that there is proof that you can send the client.

Again, our goal with our clients is that they clean the dishes and run the dishes through the dishwasher. They don't have to put them away but they do need to run the washer. We ask that they strip the beds and put one load of wash in the washer; usually the towels because they take longer to dry. We also ask that they take their garbage down to the street as well. Therefore, if the dishes are running, the garbage is all picked up, the linens are off the beds and clearly the guest has picked up all their belongings and shoved them back into their suitcase then that is a pretty easy scenario for my cleaner to take care of from there, usually.

185.

Again it's important to lay out in your contract what the guest is expected to do at checkout, it can be a real mess for your cleaner to deal with when the guest doesn't follow through. It's also, by the way, important for your cleaner to let you know right away so that you can let the guest know right away. As you can imagine you cannot bill a client a month later when you get your bill from your cleaner. It has to be done immediately. And very simply you need to charge the client for the added time. Sometimes the client will be amenable and simply understand that they woke up late, were hung-over and didn't have a chance to do stuff. Not having read the rules is never an excuse for having broken the rules. Just simply be fair with the client. If the clean took an extra hour then charge the client your cleaner's hourly rate. There is no need for "punitive damages" here necessarily. Oftentimes it will be the best $40 or $80 that the client ever spent not having to lift a finger as they check out.

Guest injuries

Knock on wood I have not had a serious guest injury at my cabin. My property is pretty steep with lots of stairs and yes I've had a few people slip on ice and snow, it's a given and most guests accept this as a fact of life at a rental property. We do not have permanent staff like a hotel would and even a hotel cannot stay ahead of the snow when it's coming down Blizzard style as it can in the mountains. You can make every preventative effort to ensure that nobody falls ever but sooner or later people fall. I usually fall at least once a week doing something or another just around my own house or even at work and I'm not very clumsy at all.

186.

The world these days seems to be filled with frivolous lawsuits but the thing that I've found is that people of class oftentimes do not sue even when they have a great reason to and I try to do a great job of providing a great rental experience at a not super cheap cost that seems to attract people of class. It's a win/win scenario. It just seems to come across to people of conscience as being the wrong thing to do. You have to remember that there is a big difference between life being imperfect and a property owner exhibiting gross negligence. Stairs that have been shoveled becoming icy overnight is the former, snow not being removed until it's four feet high is gross negligence. Clearly you can see the difference.

But what do you do if somebody does fall and it's serious enough for them to bring it to your attention. Now there might be all kinds of rules about this but I'm just going to suggest what I would do and you can make your own choices in this regard.

Obviously you need to be concerned and you need to ask the client how they are and if they physically injured themselves. Do they have a bruise, a cut, a scratch? Did they seek medical help? Again luckily for me all of my clients have said that it was minor and they are fine and not to worry. But if somebody is hurt you should probably offer them your condolences, let them know to take care of themselves to the full extent that they feel they should and then after having had that conversation call your attorney and your insurance company if they are in the office and have them deal directly with the client.

I've never had any serious falls. I mean as human beings things happen. Babies just learning to walk must fall a hundred times a day. As humans we are designed to fall and to be able to sustain the injuries associated with a fall. The only real issue that I have really ever had regarding a "guest Injury" (per se) was a client who claimed to have gotten a skin irritation from my hot tub.

187.

They had gone to the emergency room and I offered to pay their medical bill for them, simple as that. It could have been an allergic reaction or they might have been in the tub for too long, who is to stay. But I offered to make it right and I asked the client to send the bill to me and I would pay it but they refused to allow me to pay the bill and to be honest I was grateful for that.

This is maybe more a life lesson then a property manager lesson but if you offer to pay people may refuse your offer to do so but if you go out of your way to try to skirt responsibility then they just might come back and try to make you pay. How you proceed is always a crap shoot but the odds, I believe, are in your favor if you step up and attempt to do the right thing.

Indemnity Insurance

When I first started out and was in the aforementioned cabin rental system run by that property management firm I was made to get a one million dollar indemnity policy. I also have my property set up in such a way that my cabin is owned by my LLC or limited liability corporation. Basically, this way, I can get sued up to the terms of my policy and probably even the value of the equity in my property (and thanks to the real estate crash of 2008 there isn't a whole bunch of equity) but because of the limited liability corporation (LLC) they wouldn't be able to sue me personally. This comes in handy in the event that the client is able to sue you for an amount that exceeds the value of your indemnity policy. Establishing an LLC is fairly complex and I would highly recommend your sitting down with an attorney to create an LLC and then to move your properties ownership into said LLC.

Your insurance company is going to probably deal with the situation from there and it is pretty standard for them to have attorneys employed by the firm or on retainer to deal with the clients directly.

The most important thing you can do is to be concerned, this will be easy. It will also be important to not be defensive and to not try to somehow put the blame back on the client for what occurred.

Also, do not start making excuses for your property or try to explain to the client how you took various steps to ensure that this wouldn't happen.

To that end it is critically important to do everything that you can to avoid injuries from happening in the first place. You have to go over your place with a fine tooth comb.

There should be no nails sticking out of anything or rusty screws sticking out of your deck. I mean, truly, you almost need to baby proof your property and not just for babies but for the client's themselves. It's also important to tell clients to wear shoes that are appropriate for the weather. High heels in a snowstorm are a recipe for disaster. Your guests need to ensure that they are exercising caution at every turn as well but in conclusion when accidents occur, and they will, step up, do the right thing and more often than not the guest will shrug off your attempts to help and handle things on their own through their insurance.

Finally after having heard the client out and apologizing, not for causing the accident but for the fact that the accident even happened, call your insurance company and lawyer and do not say another thing until they tell you to. In these moments you have the right to remain silent and most likely you probably should.

189.

General complaint by guest

This next one isn't so much a problem with a guest but more so what to do for clients when you've made a general mistake on your end. This can range from not giving the clients the proper code to get through the door to your cleaner not having enough time between guests to clean as thoroughly as the guest would have liked (this does happen, especially during December when the cabin is booked out almost every single night.) If you end up with a late check out on top of it the arriving client might have to choose between checking in later or dealing with an imperfect cabin.

When these things occur I usually either provide the clients with a refund of a portion of their cleaning deposit or a bottle of wine or a discount on a future stay or there's always the option of letting the cleaner come back the next day, when they are out enjoying the sights, to finish up. The secret here is to gauge the situation and the level of the client's frustration and then act accordingly. But always work to find a way to make the client happy. If you always give 100% to your client there really isn't any situation that isn't fixable. Although, as we all know, .001% of the worlds population will never be happy and that is just the way that that is going to go, luckily these people are rare.

Spa Tips and Pointers and issues

As I mentioned earlier one of the greatest attractions for guests is a hot tub. It seems that when people go looking for a vacation rental one of the most important deal makers or breakers is whether or not you have one. A hot tub can also create a high degree of complaints. Hot tubs are tricky little devils that require a ton of work and maintenance.

190.

Although not even your significant other would probably consider getting in your bath water once you've gotten out of it literally millions of people every year pile into hot tubs either together or in a series of parties of people, one after the other.

There have been times when we've looked at the hot tub water after a guest stay and just knew it was time to dump it and do a a refill (not a big deal at my cabin since I'm on a well and I don't pay for the water). There are other times when guests check out and it's sparkling clean. Under normal conditions a little water balancing, a cap of shock, some clarifier and a few tabs of bromine can get the spa looking good as new but not always. Still, after all this time the financial reward for having a hot tub is too great not to have one and I know for myself, I get in my hot tub all the time upon arriving at my cabin.

To continue, if you are going to have one it is of course important that you maintain it at a very high level and if guests are going to be there for quite some time (a week or so) you need to provide people with the tools to be able to maintain it themselves.

A great suggestion right out of the gate is that you look into purchasing the Spa Frog Floating system. Instead of being highly chlorinated it's more of a mineral and bromine system that lasts for a very, very long time, usually about 6 months. After each guest we will still throw in some extra bromine and some clarifier, we will use a pool strainer to pull out any flotsam and we will also pull out the spa's filters and hose them off. But generally speaking with the Frog system you aren't going to run into a situation where the bromine or chlorine is all gone and has completely broken down and the water has a high level of bacteria content. If this occurs then your guests are going to be susceptible to spa rash which is kind of unpleasant and itchy. Additionally, most guests not knowing what it is typically will end up at the Dr. wondering what they've contracted.

191.

If you aren't going to run the Frog system then you have to provide the clients with back up bromine floaters so that if one runs out they can throw another one in. It's also a good idea to leave the guests extra clarifier and perhaps a handful of shock, just in case. If people don't have a hot tub and don't understand them they are going to confuse clean looking water with bacteria free water and that can sometimes not be the case.

Conversely if the water has some sand on the bottom (which is a common occurrence) they can sometimes confuse that with dirty water which it also is not so it's important to spell that out in your arrival letter otherwise you might get calls and complaints that your spa is dirty when it isn't.

It is also a good idea to have a list of Spa Rules next to the hot tub. These can often be found online but they should start off with the basic rules like showering before entering the spa, and no hot tubbing while pregnant or intoxicated. After that you should give client specifics about your hot tub.

For example one of the things that we often deal with is when we show up at the cabin and the spa is very cloudy. Spa cloudiness can be caused by any number of things but the general guess is that it's the simple remnants of humanity. When we do the clean at the cabin we treat the spa, we check the water balance and we then clarify it and brominate it to kill all the germs and bacteria. While the clairifier is working it's binding all of this stuff together and eventually it's going to wind up somewhere and normally it's a ring around the tub. Sometimes when my guests arrive at the cabin they find a spoonful of sand at the bottom of the tub, perfectly clear water and a spa ring and they panic thinking it's dirty. It's not dirty, it's actually very clean and all that needs to be done is to wipe the ring out of the tub and jump in. Therefore that is one of the things that is important for me to spell out in the Spa Rules and Information sheet.

If guests don't understand this they can become upset, so seeing it written out beforehand and laminated on the side of the Spa shed can alleviate all those concerns immediately.

In conclusion, there are dozens of other things that can happen to you when you decide to run your property on your own. Running into problems while running your property though is kind of like bartending. 98% of bartending is cracking beers, pouring wine and making a gin and tonic or vodka and Red bull. 2% of the time it's making Pink Squirrels or an Old Fashioned. It's the same when running a property, 98% of the time it's one of the several issues above or some other crazy thing you couldn't believe could ever happen. But you patiently listen, commiserate, tell them it will be OK. Throw some money at the problem, fix it, make it right and keep the client in your property, keep your revenue from that stay in your checking account and keep the client coming back again and again. I personally do not need things to go perfect all the time, but when something does go wrong I want to know it's going to be taken care of. That is the thing that keeps me coming back and continuing to patronize a business. (except for those who give bad haircuts, bad haircuts can ruin your life for, like, two weeks).

11

My property timeline

Now that I've explained almost all that I've learned throughout the years I thought it would be important for you to understand what my timeline has been like since purchasing my cabin. As you can see it's been a rollercoaster ride to be sure. There were the beginning stages where I understood little to nothing about owning a cabin let alone operating one. I needed to quickly integrate myself in the community, hire a company to run my place and start bringing in revenue. There were bumps in the road and even a time when I was desperate to get out of the cabin rental business, however, as fate would have it maintaining ownership of the property worked out in the long run and thankfully I never did find a buyer for my place when things got really rough, proving that sometimes fate will intervene to allow something not so great to occur so that something even better can happen down the road.

So here now is the timeline which will give you a better understanding of the road that I traveled along. My hope is that with this book your ride will be much smoother than mine but even if it's not then at least you will know that there is always light at the end of the tunnel even when you cannot see it.

August 2007 – I identified the property I wanted to buy. I took a second equity line of credit off of my primary residence for the down payment and also took a 401k loan to pay to get the place cleaned, remodeled, painted, landscaped and furnished. What great timing too, right? By next year the second equity loan would have not have been a possibility due to the downturn in the real estate market additionally if you understand the workings of a 401k loan, I took the money out at the height of the stock market and have been dollar cost averaging that money back into the market ever since, so that simply worked out brilliantly. It wasn't preconceived or premeditated brilliance it just turned out that way.

The down payment at the time was $43,000 or 10% of the property value being that it was a second home and based on fairly lax underwriting standards at the time (it might be 20-25% down at this particular time in history as the pendulum swings both ways). The total cost to furnish and repair was approximately around $15,000. The hot tub (used) was around $4000 and in the 11th hour I decided to bite the bullet and have the driveway paved which cost an extra $20,000.

What this all boiled down to was that I was going to have a new mortgage at $2,700 a month (30 year mortgage fixed at 5.75%) which covered principal, interest, taxes and insurance. I was going to have a $550 dollar a month second mortgage payment. I was going to have a $380 a month 401k loan payment.

195.

All told I was going to be looking at around $3,600 dollars a month. Now had I purchased this place two years later I probably would have only had to shell out about $2,600 dollars a month but I also would have never gotten the second equity line of credit from my first property (because, suddenly, there was no equity) and I also would have been subject to much higher lending standards and possibly a lower income due to the stock market's decimation. Therefore hindsight being 20/20 it all worked out simply as well as it could have.

September 2007 – I closed on the property and began the remodel.

Late September 2007 – The driveway was finished.

October 2007 – I placed my cabin in a property management system and got my first renter. They were the first to write complimentary things in my cabin guest register! Their only slightly negative comment was that a hot tub would really complete the place.

Early October 2007 – I bit the bullet and purchased a hot tub.

December 2007 – Due to the high demand of rentals in Leavenworth my cabin sells out all available weekends for the first time ever.

October 2007-July 2008 – Cabin managed and operated by a third party "vacation rental" property manager. As mentioned in detail this ended up working out terribly but at least I knew that I had a desirable property on my hands based on the sheer number of bookings that I was getting.

July 2008-December 2008 – Hired my second property manager who was also managing her own property and a few others as well. Revenue increased slightly as expenses declined but towards the end of her tenure I would be robbed for the first time ending our relationship.

January 2009-June 2009 – Hired a new property manager to run my place which also was a referral from the real estate company that I had hired to help me find my property. Our relationship fizzled due to issues with a double booking but she did introduce me to Vacation Rental by Owner and showed me that it was possible to handle the bookings on my own.

June 2009 – April 2010 Began to slowly become successful running the cabin myself. Came up with a dozen or more innovations to continue to streamline my rental process to include:

- Adding a buy now button to my website.
- Turning my payment instructions, arrival letter and contract into one Word/PDF document on my website.
- Getting my property onto the VRBO site.
- Determining that it made more sense to hold security deposits as opposed to depositing them into my checking account.
- I moved all of my cabin guest book comments onto my VRBO site. Adding the keypad lock and getting the alarm system up and running.

April 2010 – Frustrated with a few slow months in a row and still struggling to dig my way out of the financial crisis of 2008 I decided to put my property up for sale, turnkey for $525,000.

Although I didn't end up with a single interested buyer I did get a few good things out of putting my place up for sale to include getting some really great pictures for my VRBO site from the photographer assigned to take pictures of my cabin for the real estate company.

Having been robbed for the second time created the desire in me to move forward with the keypad lock and the surveillance system, I do believe that between the keypad lock, alarm and surveillance cameras that I finally have in place a security system that protects me from individuals who are considering robbing my property again. I ended up keeping my property on the market for a year and during that year I experienced the most explosive sales growth in the history of my cabin ownership.

April 2010-April 2011 - My property finally turned the corner and my revenue simply exploded upwards. Suddenly I found myself most months at double cash flow and in some month's triple cash flow which was just amazing considering all that my cabin, the economy and myself personally had been through over the last 3 years up to that point. I was also able, at this time, to get a HAMP refinance. (Home affordable modification program). I will tell you that once you've received a HARP refinance (making homes affordable program) which I had done, getting a HAMP refinance on a second property is a piece of cake. What this refinance was able to do for me was to turn my 5/1 option arm that I was paying 5.75% on into a 30 year fixed mortgage at 5.125%. Now that this is accomplished if interest rates rise in the future I won't find myself paying 6% to 11% or more on my mortgage, a real win/win for both the bank and myself.

April 2011-today - Cash flow continues to be fantastic. Most months I find myself booked out some 20-25+ days per month. At 180 dollars a night on average I'm bringing in $4000-$5000 dollars per month. My goal every month is to make both of my mortgage payments from my cabin revenue. Being that those are the two largest checks that I write each month and if I can get those covered than everything else is paid for from my income at work.

198.

It's a good feeling to be in sales and in a profession where I set my own hours to a point and where I don't have to rely only on the income that my employer provides me.

The cabin remains running very smoothly now. My cleaner is the best in the business and handles all of the day to day intricacies of being a hands on cleaner and in town manager. I merely find myself these days contacting those interested in renting my cabin, negotiating deals for them and taking in funds.

12

Bringing it Home / Glimpsing the Future

In conclusion owning and running your own vacation rental property can be highly rewarding, highly educational, financially enriching and all the while still providing you and your family a great place to hang your hat whenever you see fit to go and spend some of your time there. In running your own property you are going to save thousands of dollars in fees that would otherwise go to somebody else who most likely isn't going to care less about how often your property gets rented so long as their bottom line is being met through the slew of properties that they are currently renting.

The tax benefits could save you thousands of dollars a year and the capital gains over the long haul could very well end up becoming a huge part of your long term financial plan. Over time if you can avoid pulling equity out of your property and if you can get your mortgage paid off without pursuing a constant stream of refinances you will experience the kind of cash flow in retirement that only few can dream of.

The price appreciation combined with the paying off of your mortgage could put you in a place where you have this very large and hopefully, at the time, liquid asset that you could either sell, keep, take an income stream from or live in. There would be so many choices for you down the road.

Having a chance to run your own business is also very rewarding and educational. The best education you will ever receive is from actually doing something. You can read all of the textbooks in the world but until you've run your own business, worked to turn a profit, sat down to pay employees and expenses and dealt with customers and inventories and so forth then that is all that you have is a vague memory of something that you've read in a book. You can read about going to France or you can go to France and I think that you will agree that those two things are very different things indeed.

With this book you now have a manual and a blueprint, you have the ability to avoid most of the mistakes that I've made but just know you will make mistakes and it's in overcoming those mistakes that you actually will grow. I could have given up on my property a dozen times and almost did once, the fact remains that if somebody had come along with a little over a half of a million dollars I may very well not be writing these words here today. Fate has a funny way of intervening though.

201.

<u>Looking into the future</u>

Although no one can really see into the future and say for certain what is going to happen to the economy, the vacation rental market or taxes as it relates to property ownership (mortgage interest deductions, depreciating your property and equipment, etc.) We can look at any number of 20 year rolling periods and attempt to glean some estimates of things like:

- What will taxes be like in the future, based on historical changes to the tax code?
- What will be the approximate rate of real estate appreciation based on historical rolling 20 year periods?
- What will inflation do to rental income moving forward based on historical precedent?

Here are some numbers that I've run for myself based upon the last 80 or so years when looking at the history of tax law changes, the economy and the real estate market.

If my property right now is worth approximately $425,000, (which is my assumed valuation based upon a recent appraisal combined with recent work that I've completed to the cabin.) And if the current rate of real estate appreciation is 4-6%. Then my cabin, in 20 years, when I get ready to retire, should be worth........ *drumroll please*........$900,000-$1.3 million dollars.

Now I know that sounds pretty wild but that is just simply math based on historical real estate appreciation rates. I certainly cannot promise that this will be the case but if things continue as they always have then there is a great chance that this could very well become the case.

Also in 20 years my cabin should be either paid off or just about paid off but even if it's not the mortgage payment should be diminutive relative to my income because although my mortgage payment will not be inflating, my income from my cabin will, therefore, based on the current rate of inflation my income in 20 years should be.....*drumroll again please*........ about $525 dollars per night or $13,125 per month if I can continue to rent my property out 20-25 days per month.

Based on these assumptions there is no wonder why most people would love to own a rental property whether it's a cabin a house in the suburbs or even an apartment building downtown. Through my career as I've taken a look into many "trust funds" or when I've had an opportunity to see how "generational wealth" is created it's created just this way - owning real estate or stocks and bonds for the long haul. You could have bought 3 rental properties in 1960 and even if two were sold or even if two were condemned you still would have made quite a sum off of the one that is still owned. Put another way you could have bought 10 stocks in 1985 and if one of those stocks was Microsoft, even if all the others had failed you'd still be a millionaire today!

Now over time there have been a number of tax law changes and every time they start talking about making changes to the tax code they always talk about getting rid of mortgage interest deductions or depreciation or phasing out or sun-setting this tax provision or that tax provision or simply moving to a flat tax. The thing that I've seen though is that if they decided to do either of those things I believe it could be disastrous for our economy and for real estate and the reasons are simple;

203.

without mortgage interest deductions it wouldn't really make sense to buy a home anymore, because really, if you pencil things out it most times would make more sense to simply rent.

However, it also might not make sense for even *real estate investors* to own rental properties either which would leave real estate in a very precarious place. So, I believe, we could see some minor adjustments over time perhaps, but sweeping changes, well, I don't really see that happening.

Additionally, if they did change to something like a flat tax we would suddenly have very little need for CPA's, the IRS, tax preparers, accountants, tax lawyers and really, simply an entire industry that has been built around the tax code. So, therefore, I don't see much happening, from a tax standpoint, that could do a lot of damage to the value of owning or buying real estate. Fingers crossed.

With all this taken into consideration, I believe that if things progress as they always have. then those who can make the sacrifices, take the risks, endure the challenges and follow these guidelines can do very, very well. The fact remains that you won't need a get rich quick scheme to become successful and you will find, in time, that get rich slow schemes work really, really well. Besides, time goes by so fast these days it might almost seem that you've gotten rich quickly!

In closing

So as I conclude I would like to add that I wish you the best of luck in your endeavors and I honestly believe that we are rewarded in life for taking chances and overcoming obstacles because if you can do those two things then there is no way that you cannot become successful.

I feel that I have done everything that I can to condense 6 years of Vacation Property ownership and management knowledge along with 15 years' worth of real estate and financial market experience into one book. I hope that I have done that. Now it is simply up to you to make it happen.

If you are interested in additional consulting or coaching please feel free to reach out to me through my website www.cabinateaglecreek.com.

Made in the USA
San Bernardino, CA
05 March 2018